Wallace Stevens

and the

Critical Schools

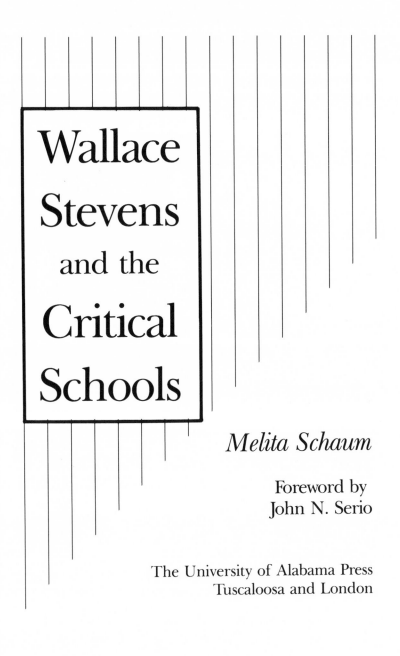

Wallace Stevens and the Critical Schools

Melita Schaum

Foreword by
John N. Serio

The University of Alabama Press
Tuscaloosa and London

The Elizabeth Agee Prize,

presented annually by

The University of Alabama Press

to honor the author of the most deserving

manuscript in the field of

American Literary Studies,

was awarded for 1987 to

Melita Schaum for *Wallace Stevens and the Critical Schools*

Copyright © 1988 by
The University of Alabama Press
Tuscaloosa, Alabama 35487
All rights reserved
Manufactured in the United States of America

Library of Congress Cataloging-in-Publication Data

Schaum, Melita, 1957–
  Wallace Stevens and the critical schools.

  Bibliography: p.
  Includes index.
  1. Stevens, Wallace, 1879–1955—Criticism and interpretation—History. 2. Criticism—United States—History—20th century. I. Title.
PS3537.T4753Z7645   1988   811'.52   87-10789
ISBN 0-8173-0374-X

British Library Cataloguing-in-Publication Data is available.

To my mother and father
for their support and love
in this, as in everything

Contents

Foreword

In the summer of 1984, I received a manuscript entitled "Concepts of Irony in Stevens' Early Critics" by Melita Schaum. Impressed with the essay's analysis of the early reviews of Wallace Stevens' poetry, I sent the manuscript off to the other members of the editorial board of *The Wallace Stevens Journal* for evaluation. Within a couple of weeks a highly favorable report came back recommending publication. The article had yet to appear in print when another essay arrived from Melita Schaum, this one on the movement in Stevens criticism from decreation to deconstruction in the seminal 1960s and 1970s. I suspected then that these incisive essays were leading to a larger project. A call to Ms. Schaum confirmed my impressions: a book was in the making. Recognizing the importance of this work to the readers of *The Wallace Stevens Journal*, I requested that we see the remaining segment of her historical overview, which dealt with the inscription of Stevens into the 1980s. I am now delighted that "the Schaum series," as it became known among our readers, has been completed in a fuller, book-length account.

Wallace Stevens' poetic career spanned the first half of this century, and critical books and articles about him, especially in the last twenty years, have increased at a seemingly exponential rate. As a poet posing more questions than answers ("One goes on asking questions. That, then, is one / Of the categories"), as a poet worrying the problematic of language in virtually every poem, Stevens has been a fertile subject for critical inquiry. Yet the literary criticism about him has been heterogeneous, contradictory, and, of late, laden with an almost impenetrable terminology. In *Wallace Stevens and the Critical Schools*, Schaum provides a clarifying framework for the plethora of Stevens criticism over the last seventy years. She defines critical theory as an agonistic activity, a clash between competing ideologies, which often makes and breaks reputations. She clusters major trends in Stevens criticism around the conflicting theoretical movements that have defined our century—aestheticism versus humanism; new humanism versus New Criticism; structuralism versus poststructuralism. Thus, just as a magnet orders iron filaments around opposing polarities, Schaum elucidates divergent critical theories by highlighting implicit patterns.

Interest in this book, therefore, extends beyond Stevens specialization, for in charting the ups and downs of various critical concepts, Schaum maps the intellectual history of twentieth-century America. Whether discussing the fierce dispute raging between Conrad Aiken and Louis Untermeyer, Witter Bynner's founding of *Spectra* (a hoax turned movement), the tension between formalism and deconstruction, or the more recent controversy between technique and meaning (classicism versus romanticism), Schaum situates the particular critical school in its historical and intellectual context. In the process, something else emerges as well, something more profound, for Schaum gives us insight into the very nature of criticism itself. After observing the rise and decline (and even resurfacing) of various critical stances, we recognize that literary theory is as changeable, fluid, and

Foreword

dynamic as the literature it addresses. Like art, the act of
interpretation is subject to a certain time, a certain place,
a certain pressure. Modifying Stevens, we could say it is
not in the premise that criticism is a solid.

Finally, Schaum's study sends us back into the poetry
of Wallace Stevens, a heartening, yet frightening turn. It
frightens us because our confidence in our own critical
response to Stevens is shaken. After witnessing the
poet's adoption by some critical schools for the very reasons given for his rejection by others, after seeing our
own interpretative bias undermined by an opposing,
equally persuasive critical theory, how can it be other-
wise? Yet, it heartens us, for we are convinced that this
poet, perhaps more than others, sustains, indeed nour-
ishes, such interpretative gestures. We realize that if major critics of our time can change their minds about
Stevens, so can we. Stimulated by Schaum's discussion of
the richly pluralistic responses to Stevens, we desire to
go back to the poetry, to see Stevens in a new light. The
result will be what Paul de Man predicted some time
ago: our original insights will become our blindness,
and our new blindness, like that of Oedipus, will be
transfigured into new insights.

So what is Wallace Stevens—dandy, hedonist, aesthete,
modernist, romantic, metaphysician, phenomenologist,
decreator, deconstructor, postmodernist, visionary,
nihilist, affirmer? They will get it straight one day at the
Sorbonne (or is it Yale?). Returning from a lecture, convinced that the irrational is rational, flicked by feeling in
a gildered street, they will flatly call him by name. But
after reading *Wallace Stevens and the Critical Schools*, we

xi

will know better. Stevens will have stopped revolving except in crystal.

Clarkson University
Potsdam, New York

John N. Serio, Editor
The Wallace Stevens Journal

Preface

An overview of seventy years of Stevens criticism shows it to be a field marked by conflict and contradiction, both within and among critical works in their attempts to explicate and appropriate this major American poet. Stevens' changing reception among the critical schools reveals much about the shifting nature of American literature and criticism in this century and illuminates the often polemical process of literary canon formation. Yet although surveys and bibliographies of Stevens criticism abound, the issue of critical trends and what they reveal is seldom addressed. Some surveys perform an excellent service in classifying Stevens criticism according to chronology or topical concerns, but while these studies bring interesting controversies to light, they fall short of analyzing the grounds for conflict and the aesthetic attitudes such critical disagreements express. Other surveys merely provide reference and bibliographical information, and the remainder, in their selection and exclusion of essays, fall into critical trends themselves and so become texts for examination.

Despite the lack of systematic overviews, Wallace Stevens lends himself especially well to a study of the changing nature of critical engagement. The length of Stevens' career; the volume and quality of his poetry and prose; his wealth of connections to fine arts, philosophy, and theory; and his extensive correspondence have made Stevens a rich vehicle for the deployment of aesthetic theories. The mass of criticism on this author from the 1910s to the present provides a formidable archive for analysis: Stevens' career spans most of the major critical movements of this century, and the vicissitudes of his emergence during the fledgling modernist period in literature illuminate the literary and critical readjustments demanded by the modern age.

An examination of the conditions of Stevens' emergence as a literary figure demands an overview of the context of avant-garde thought and expression in which he began publishing during the early decades of the twentieth century, a paradoxical milieu of rebellion against and courting of established artistic institutions. The early modernist movement was a phenomenon which elicited Stevens' ambivalence from the time of his earliest publications, yet also involved him in the melee of affiliations and enmities, tags and labels that characterized the fluid literary scene. Early criticism of Stevens' work shows mixed, often controversial responses—not surprisingly during a time when vers libre itself was an issue arousing the questioning and readjustment of poetic standards. The major conflicts over Stevens and other modern poets during the 1910s and 1920s indicate an essential antithesis between ideologies which advocated relativity in evaluation and skepticism in thought and those which underwrote a fundamental faith in human and universal stability. The crux of contention between the "aesthetic" and the "humanist" positions in early criticism of Stevens revolves around the issue of irony, as that concept gradually took its place in the modern critic's general repertoire. The penetration of conventional views of the world, language, art, and self became the frame within which Stevens was polemically either invoked or condemned.

In 1930 the confrontation between the new humanists and young formalist critics such as Allen Tate, R. P. Blackmur, and Edmund Wilson created a new turn in criticism, which attempted to recover poetry from both the dogmatic rigidity of new humanism and the overly impressionistic dangers of aesthetic subjectivism. The "New Criticism," based as it was on the autonomy of the art form and the uniqueness of aesthetic experience, sought to employ Stevens' work as an argument in support of organic form, artistic autotelism, or a more aesthetic brand of secular humanism. The 1930s, 1940s, and 1950s were decades during which Stevens criticism was dominated by such critics as Louis Martz, Robert Lowell, Randall Jarrell, Edmund Wilson, Donald Davie, William Empson, Allen Tate, T. S. Eliot, John Crowe Ransom, and Frank Kermode. But while critical consensus declared Stevens a major figure to be dealt with, contradictions and conflicts abounded over Stevens' place in the canon of American literature. The emphasis on resolution and closure in poetry—whether formalist, humanist, or metaphysical—was everywhere evident in explications of Stevens' poetry, causing greater and greater concern as Stevens' work progressed to the difficult late poems.

Beginning in the 1960s, the careers of critics like Joseph Riddel and J. Hillis Miller have occasioned still further turns in Stevens criticism, attempts to dislodge Stevens from his position in the New Critical framework by inscribing him into a poststructuralist context. Dealing with the issue of rupture in Stevens' late poetry, examinations of the works began to resituate the structure and function of the poetry according to radical and innovative standards. Growing critical concentration on themes and instances of absence, decreation, non-sense, flux, and the surface play of language in Stevens seeks to compete for the appropriation of this poet as a figure anticipating postmodern issues and concerns.

The turns in critical theory continue today, redesigning the hierarchy of literary values, often redefining the very concept of modernism. Deconstruction itself has proved a battleground over which theories compete; critics continue to use Stevens as inspiration for and illustration of new directions in literary polemics. This book aims neither to achieve a definitive closure nor to resolve contradictions in critical discourse but to identify and explore those conflicts and discontinuities which emerge in the ongoing debate over Wallace Stevens' place in American letters. Stevens' works remain texts around which criticism engages in its recurrent revolutions, a literary *arena*—as that word denotes "a clearing for struggle, conflict, play"—in which major critical assumptions continue to be determined and debated.

Parts of this work were published in *The Wallace Stevens Journal,* and my gratitude to its editor, John Serio, runs deep. A sensitive scholar and impeccable businessman (a combination most fitting in a follower of Stevens), he gave generous doses of personal and professional support that have been invaluable both in the development of the book and in the start of my career.

Preface

I acknowledge with thanks publishers' permission to quote from the following sources: from *Literature and Belief,* edited by M. H. Abrams, copyright 1958 by Columbia University Press; from *Wallace Stevens: The Poetics of Modernism,* edited by Albert Gelpi, copyright 1985 by Cambridge University Press; from *After the New Criticism* by Frank Lentricchia, copyright 1980 by University of Chicago Press and The Athlone Press, London; from "Bloom—A Commentary—Stevens" and "The Climate of Our Poems" by Joseph Riddel, copyright 1977 and 1983 respectively, by *The Wallace Stevens Journal;* from "Interpreting Stevens: An Essay on Poetry and Thinking" by Joseph Riddel, copyright 1972 by *boundary 2;* from *Men Seen: Twenty-Four Modern Authors* by Paul Rosenfeld, copyright 1925 by The Dial Press/Doubleday & Company, Inc.; from *The Act of the Mind: Essays on the Poetry of Wallace Stevens* edited by Roy Harvey Pearce and J. Hillis Miller, copyright 1965 by Johns Hopkins University Press; from *The Spectra Hoax* by William Jay Smith, copyright 1961 by Wesleyan University Press; and from *Harriet Monroe and the Poetry Renaissance* by Ellen Williams, copyright 1977 by The Board of Trustees of the University of Illinois.

In addition, I am indebted to the University of Notre Dame for the yearlong research fellowship which saw this project through its first phases and to the University of Michigan–Dearborn for a subsequent Campus Grant and Research Assistance Award, which provided support for work on Chapter 5. A summer at The School of Criticism and Theory at Northwestern University helped sharpen my later thoughts on Stevens, and for that I have particularly to thank Frank Lentricchia, as excellent a teacher as he is a scholar, and indirectly Geoffrey Hartman, the guiding spirit of The School of Criticism.

Of special value were the friends and colleagues who gave their time and encouragement during the growth of this book from its infancy: my thanks in particular to John Matthias, Joseph Duffy, and Stephen Fredman for their intellectual obstetrics during the project's birth; to Chris Dahl, Claude Summers, Neil Flax, and Alan Golding for reading parts of the manuscript; to Jeff Peter for research assistance; and to Claudia Bayliss and Jackie Lawson for friendship and inspiration then and now.

I reserve a special word of thanks for Joseph Buttigieg—teacher, mentor, and more—who for four years made me answer the questions and question the answers and who showed me the way . . . by letting me find it for myself.

Wallace Stevens and the Critical Schools

1

He came. *The poetic hero without palms*
Or jugglery, without regalia.
—Wallace Stevens

I Am What Is
around Me:
The Emergence
of a Poet

The twentieth-century avant-garde was a movement dependent on energy and opposition, an activism reflective of the modern cult of speed and dynamism, channeled into an antagonism toward convention, tradition, and the past. As such, it stood as a phenomenon pitted against all symbols of modern homogeneity: mass production, commercialization, the deadening unselectivity of bourgeois minds. "I grow infinitely weary of accepting things," wrote Wallace Stevens as early as 1904. "I sicken of patterns, and trite symbols, and conventions and the lack of thought" (Stevens, *Letters* 79). And Stevens was only one voice clamoring for newness and individuality amid the "noise—noise—noise" of the emerging twentieth-century artistic revolt (Stevens, *Letters* 50).

The energy fueling vanguard twentieth-century art was a transgressive energy, a realizing and surpassing of limits and "norms," a revitalization dependent on anarchy and action. Like a gestalt figure and ground, its emergence from and contrast to nineteenth-century Victorian stolidity afforded a startling sense of its urgency and excess. Publications with violent, antagonistic names like *Blast, Damn, Exile, Fugitive, Pagan, Experiment, Secession;* Marcel Duchamp's "explosion in a shingle factory," John Dos Passos' "explosion in a cesspool," Tristan Tzara's "explosion of the past" and "explosion of the future" illustrated the energy and urgency of the movement. In Russia, Vladimir Mayakovsky wrote, "Make bombardment echo on the museum walls" and "I write *nihil* on anything that has been done before"; and Tzara in Vienna: "There is a great destructive, negative task to be done: sweeping out, cleaning up." Both sentiments find accord with Ezra Pound's manifesto in the vorticist publication *Blast,* whose task, he declared, was "to make the rich of the community shed their education skin, to destroy politeness, standardization and academic, that is civilized, vision." Combined, the international drive for originality and revitalization was out to make short work of Arnoldian drawing-room serenity and the anemia of nineteenth-century art.

In America the avant-garde presented a "renaissance" in letters, the pure energy of which was absorbed fairly quickly but which brought on its crest some of the major artistic figures of the twentieth century, along with radical movements which were redirecting the course of modern poetry and criticism. It was into this milieu of violence and novelty that Wallace Stevens emerged, moving to New York, finding a forum for his poetry in Greenwich Village magazines, accompanying his contemporaries to the Armory Show of 1913, or circulating, a silent and by all reports imposing man, among chinoiserie and abstract art at vanguard New York salon parties. Stevens' move from the classrooms of Harvard to the bohemian Village invites an easy contrast between a stuffy, classical background and a liberation into the world of bluestockings and red scares. But in fact, Harvard during Stevens' attendance (1897–90) was a fairly liberal institution, housing such diverse and often antagonistic minds as Irving Babbitt and George Santayana. Although Stevens' curriculum included traditional courses of study like "English Literature to Tennyson," his professor of English, Charles Townsend Copeland, had connections with such Greenwich Village radicals as Jack Reed and staged Saturday evening sessions in his bachelor quarters at Harvard, during which "startling theories" and "strange systems of philosophy" were discussed in a casual atmosphere (Humphrey 127). We can judge the ambiance of turn-of-the-century Harvard by Irving Babbitt's impetuous call for its reform in his 1908 tract *Literature and the American College:*

> Our educators, in their anxiety not to thwart native aptitudes, encourage the individual in an in-breeding of his own temperament, which, beginning in kindergarten, is carried upward through the college by the elective system, and receives its final consecration in his specialty. We are all invited to abound in our own sense, and to fall in the direction in which we lean. Have we escaped from the pedantry of authority and prescription, which was the bane of the old education, only to

3

lapse into the pedantry of individualism? (Babbitt 93–94)

It seems that Stevens was receiving the better part of this training in individualism, so subversive to classical tradition. At Harvard, too, he formed friendships with a number of young men who would later assist his emergence: Witter Bynner, Arthur Davison Ficke, Walter Arensberg, and Pitts Sanborn.

Stevens' writing during his Harvard years—published in the *Harvard Advocate,* where he served as literary editor from 1898 on—although competent, shows little real experimentation or innovation. A number of images to be elaborated in later works do appear in these early poems, but in general Stevens' Harvard poems reflect, as Robert Buttel points out, merely the prevailing nineteenth-century themes and styles, echoing the Pre-Raphaelites, Tennyson, Keats, Fitzgerald. Buttel writes: "The language of poetry had by the end of the century fallen into a conventional literary style. . . . Stevens during this period had no particularly original point of view which demanded original means of expression. . . . most of these [early] poems are essentially exercises in the current modes" (Buttel 11).

Fourteen years passed between Stevens' college years and his emergence in Village magazines—years during which he moved to New York, attempted a career in newspaper journalism, entered law school, and began to establish himself in the insurance business. Stevens continued to read extensively, form opinions on philosophy and aesthetics, and meet with his Harvard-now-Village

4

friends Bynner and Arensberg. His journal entries of
this time show an eclecticism and idiosyncracy of material and opinion which cannot but fulfill Babbitt's expectations of dilettantism. Stevens enjoyed Matthew Arnold
and the Chinese poet Wang An-shih, Thackeray and the
French symbolists; he expressed an ambivalent distaste,
then admiration for the often-missed impressionistic
side of humanist Paul Elmer More, praising More's view
of nature as feminine, mysterious, illusory.

Stevens' thoughts on modern art during this time
show a desire for novelty and originality, yet reveal a
strange reticence toward the theories of his contemporaries. About traditional artists like Coleridge he wrote,
"It is heavy work, reading things like that, that have so
little in them that one feels to be contemporary, living"
(Stevens, *Letters* 121). Regarding the attitude of his own
age toward poetry, Stevens regretted that "with the
growth of criticism both in understanding and influence, poetry for poetry's sake, 'debonaire and gentle' has
become difficult. The modern conception of poetry is
that it should be in the service of something, as if Beauty
was not something quite sufficient when in no other service than its own" (Stevens, *Letters* 147). And yet, Stevens
was strangely coy about the more radical theories of the
avant-garde, writing of his poet friend Witter Bynner,
"He has gathered his own impressions + odd ones they
are" (Stevens, *Letters* 71), and later making similar statements about the works and ideas of such artists as Marcel Duchamp. It was a hesitancy which would carry on
through Stevens' future connections with the avant-
garde, making him a complex, almost paradoxical fig-

ure of affiliation with and segregation from contemporary movements. About his own writing, Stevens was less ambivalent. He was indeed writing during this time, having made the resolution "to write something every night—be it no more than a line to sing to or a page to read—there's gold there for the digging: j'en suis sur" (Stevens, *Letters* 62). To his future wife, Elsie Viola Moll, he wrote, "I should like to make a music of my own, a literature of my own, and I should like to live my own life" and "One of my ideals is to make everything expressive, and thus true. I would like to get out of line" (Stevens, *Letters* 79, 80). Although the poetry he compiled during these years resulted only in two private pamphlets of poems to his wife, it was out of these collections—the "June Book" of 1908 and the "Little June Book" of 1909—that Stevens drew poems to appear as parts of his first Greenwich Village publication, the "Carnet de Voyage" sequence in the September 1914 issue of *Trend* magazine.

Stevens' publication in *Trend* marked his entry into the fascinating and distinctly avant-garde small magazine movement in America of the 1910s and 1920s. The phenomenon of the "little magazine" was itself a reaction against conventional, mass-produced literature. These avant-garde reviews springing up throughout Europe and America were small, infrequently published, selective, and antagonistic to bourgeois audiences and popular taste. Indeed, the terms "public taste" and "bourgeois culture" were taken as oxymorons by many of these vanguard intellectual and artistic publications. Their editorial policies of opposition to the public were evident in the title of the Russian futurist publication *A Whack at Public Taste;* in *transition*'s manifesto, which boasted, "The plain reader be damned"; or in the slogan of Margaret Anderson's *Little Review,* which read, "Making no compromise with public taste."

Renato Poggioli compares the little magazine to its enemy, the larger popular journal, which "satisfies the crowd's passions and the crowd compensates it with an immense circulation and a notable economic success. On the other hand, the triumph of mass journalism is precisely what motivates and justifies the existence of the avant-garde review, which represents a reaction, as natural as it is necessary, to the spread of culture out to (or down to) the vulgar" (Poggioli 23). In spirit and practice, then, these publications allied themselves with the concept of the new: they served as forums for manifestos of thought and opinion or as small, sporadic anthologies exhibiting the work of vanguard artists. Whether by intent or by accident, however, these journals often became coteries, categories, labels by which poets were grouped, handles by which the works of individual authors might begin to be sorted and mastered. The element of affiliation was and remains a powerful factor in criticism and evaluation. Stevens' links to various avant-garde organs served to confuse early critics in their attempts to situate him.

When Stevens' Harvard friend Pitts Sanborn became editor of *Trend* early in 1914, the magazine became an "aggressively modernist" review, presenting a forum for the work of such controversial writers as Donald Evans, Djuna Barnes, Mina Loy, Carl Van Vechten, and Walter

Conrad Arensberg, along with Stevens. This first group of writers, in whose company Stevens emerged, was to influence both his reception and the future forums for his early work. Carl Van Vechten took over editorship of *Trend* during the next two issues, publishing his poems "From a Junk" and "Home Again" in November 1914. Van Vechten, the man who would eventually "cajole Alfred Knopf into printing Harmonium" (Kreymborg, *Strength* 500), gives us perhaps the most vivid record of the excitement of affiliation and the drive to form poetic schools and their periodicals during this time. In his memoir of 1914, "Rogue Elephant in Porcelain," Van Vechten recalls joint efforts with Arensberg to induce Stevens and a number of other poets to form a new poetic movement:

> One day the idea of the post-decadents occurred to me. I had been reading over George Moore's *Vale* and, coming upon AE's description of a literary movement, "five or six men who live in the same town and hate each other," I thought that the group of poets with whom my life at this time seemed more or less connected certainly formed a literary movement. . . . It seemed to me that these poets could much better face their contemporaries and posterity as a movement. The spires would rise, but it was necessary to erect a mountain to build them on, a term which should be at once a reproach and a stimulant and, best of all, an easy tag. . . .
>
> Walter Arensberg had been talking a great deal at this time, especially with Donald Evans, of starting a small magazine in which they and others of us might express ourselves. . . .

8

Emergence of a Poet

It occurred to me that this magazine would be an excellent medium for the exploitation of the post-decadent movement. The names rapidly came into my mind: Donald Evans, Allen Norton, Walter Arensberg (who wrote as differently as possible from the others but who, still, knew them and in a sense worked with them, and who certainly was in sympathy with them), Louise Norton, and Wallace Stevens. I was to be the biographer of the movement. (Van Vechten 45–47)

Although the "post-decadents" never quite congealed as a movement—nor did plans for the periodical, titled *New Moon* and advertised with typical avant-garde antagonism as "not for sale for 50 cents"—the coterie had been established, particularly the working bond between Stevens and Walter Arensberg.

At Harvard, Arensberg had been described as the young man "who knew all that was to be known about Pater" (Lafferty 113). Now, as a figure in Greenwich Village of the 1910s, he seemed an axle whose spokes extended to nearly every new movement: symbolism, imagism, dadaism, surrealism. "His interest [in fellow artists] amounted to excitement," wrote Wallace Stevens in later years. "He was just the man to become absorbed in cubism and in everything that followed" (Stevens, *Letters* 821–22). Alfred Kreymborg, too, remarked that Arensberg "made each movement his own . . . Symbolism, Imagism, Vorticism, Cubism, Dadaism" (Kreymborg, *Strength* 467). If Stevens can be said to have had a link to the more radical movements of the age, Arensberg may well have been that early connection.

Arensberg was among those excited about the February 17, 1913, Armory Show, the revolutionary exhibition which included Continental avant-garde artists Duchamp, Picasso, Braque, Van Gogh, and Gaugin. The highly controversial show spurred such comments as those of Princeton art historian Frank Jewett Mather, Jr., who urged the viewer to "dismiss on moral grounds an art that lives in the miasma of morbid hallucination or sterile experimentation and denies in the name of individualism values which are those of society and life itself," or Theodore Roosevelt's equally ardent view of Duchamp's celebrated *Nude Descending a Staircase* that it was a "picture of a misshapen nude woman repellent from every point of view" (Humphrey 16). Nonetheless, "there was no one for whom the Armory Show meant more" than for Arensberg, according to Stevens. Arensberg "took up" Duchamp, as he took up other revolutionary artists and their theories, and it was said that New York dada found its headquarters in Arensberg's living room (Tashjian 56). It was through Arensberg that Stevens met Duchamp, although he wrote to his wife that when he "looked at some of Duchamp's things" in Arensberg's apartment, then doubling as a studio for Duchamp, he "made very little out of them" (Stevens, *Letters* 185).

Although Stevens' contact with more radical aesthetics continued, so too did his ambivalence. In January 1917 he published the sequence "Primordia" in Robert Coady's magazine *Soil,* a publication which advocated avant-garde policies of immediacy and at-hand materials under the heading of an "American" art. Examples are Coady's "Moving Sculpture Series," which displayed as art such industrial items as jib cranes, locomotives, forging presses, and mechanical hammers. *Soil* offered articles on the Woolworth Building, the Bronx Zoo, the dime novel as literature, and prizefighters Jack Johnson, Jack Dillon, Kid Lewis, and "Battling" Levinsky—all in a context of American aesthetics. Alongside the work of artists Jean Crotti and Picasso stood such visual puns as "Which Is the Monument?" showing side-by-side plates of the Maine Monument and a Chambersburg Double Frame Steam Hammer, strikingly similar in form. The dadaist influences of immediacy, direct presentation, and ready-made materials were also reflected in such tendenz publications as *Secession* and *Broom,* under the direction of Matthew Josephson and Malcolm Cowley; both magazines provided exposure for the work of Stevens. *Broom,* much like *Soil,* promised "to welcome 'the challenging American scene,' machine and all: skyscrapers, jazz, dime novels, cowboy movies and the like" (Tashjian 74).

William Carlos Williams, too, provided publicity—along with much advice—for Stevens, attempting through their long association to "discipline" what he saw as Stevens' imagistic tendencies, excising the "pure bunk" and praising the "fervor" of various poems. Williams pleaded in a letter of June 8, 1916, to a somewhat unresponsive Stevens: "For Christ's sake yield to me, become great and famous!" But their correspondence continued as a polite tug-of-war for years, each poet respecting the other's accomplishments but Stevens resisting Williams' ventures, including the "Contact aesthetic," developed in the early twenties and carried out in the four-issue periodical *Contact*. Begun in 1920 by Williams and Robert McAlmon, the Contact aesthetic emphasized discovery, pure sense perception, and contact with the local American environment. Williams also toyed with the dadaist concept of tension between anti-poetic and poetic. "To a man with a sentimental side," wrote Stevens ten years later, "the anti-poetic is that truth, that reality to which all of us are forever fleeing." However, Stevens did publish poetry in *Contact* during its short life-span and remained affiliated with Williams for many years.

If Stevens rubbed shoulders with dada/tendenz writing, he also came in touch with another early literary trend virtually antithetical to the radical experimentation of dada. Again, it was Walter Conrad Arensberg who was responsible for Stevens' introduction to the small magazine circle of Allen and Louise Norton and their New York publication *Rogue*. Carl Van Vechten recalls the "conspiracy" of a dinner party arranged at Arensberg's apartment for the purpose of drawing Stevens out from his quiet home life and into more of the Village poetic circles. It was at this party, attended by the Nortons, that Stevens read a number of poems, including "Cy Est Pourtraicte, Madame Ste Ursule, et Les Unze Mille Vierges," which was not only received with delight but was published soon after in *Rogue* (Van Vechten 48). But in *Rogue* and its artists we find another tendency exhibited in some new movements—a somewhat dandyish aestheticism, a love for chinoiserie and languid elegance, an echo of Wilde and the decadents which later earned them the epithet "Exquisites" (Buttel

12

82). Alfred Kreymborg mentions the emergence and character of the magazine in his autobiography: "A lively paper called Rogue appeared in the village, smacking of the 1890's in London" (Kreymborg, *Troubadour* 218).

Donald Evans provides an example of the *Rogue* artist, "enchanted" with what Buttel calls "highly civilized, even rococo, ritual in an atmosphere of feminine beauty and gorgeous decor" (Buttel 91). Buttel traces Stevens' proximity to Evans in certain poems, titles, and lines. The question of influence, however, is less central here than the general stylistic affiliation among these poets and the "easy tag" of dandy, aesthete, and "gloved and monocled" spectator which adhered to Stevens in some early critical estimations. Even Louise Norton's self-conscious parody of decadent aesthetic languor in her play *Little Wax Candle* (1914) could satirize but not soften the "exquisite" aestheticism of this literary circle.

Although literary affiliation sometimes made for support—following Van Vechten's analogy of the spires of individual talent rising from the "mountain" of a supportive literary group—often the critics failed to see the spires for the mountain itself, especially when that mountain was one insurmountably hostile to the critic. *Trend* was one of the magazines whose poets, Stevens included, suffered this type of criticism-by-proxy, by virtue of a number of editorial attacks and rebuttals aimed at contemporary critics. An essay by Pitts Sanborn published in *Trend* in 1916 accused, among others, critic and poet Louis Untermeyer of being a sheer "noisemaker" and reactionary in an age of poetic progress. The attack may have helped aggravate Untermeyer's notable antagonism toward many modernist artists, which came out vehemently in his later American anthologies, his critical debates, and his stridently neohumanistic essays against modernism. Stevens, too, found himself in the good company of T. S. Eliot and Ezra Pound on Untermeyer's blacklist.

Sanborn's essay also trod on the toes of another poet, Stevens' own friend Witter Bynner, who was similarly accused of conservatism in his poetry. This cut by *Trend* narrowly preceded one of the more amusing offshoots of literary history, in which Stevens was marginally involved. William Jay Smith, in *The Spectra Hoax,* traces the history of one of the most astonishing hoaxes in literature, devised and successfully carried out for two years by Witter Bynner and Arthur Davison Ficke, later joined by Chicago poet Marjorie Allen Seiffert. Under the aliases of Emanuel Morgan, a sulky ex-painter from Paris; Anne Knish, a "devastatingly beautiful" Budapest-born critic and poet; and the "briefless barrister" Elijah Hay, the three launched the Spectric school, a wildly parodic statement against the poetic fads permeating the literary scene.

Smith describes the evening in February 1916 when the concept of Spectra was born. Bynner, on his way to visit Ficke in Davenport, Iowa, stopped in Chicago, where, in the company of friends, he attended a performance of *Le Spectre de la rose:*

> During the intermission . . . Mr. Bynner discussed with his friends the absurdity of some of the recent "schools."

14

Emergence of a Poet

There were the Imagists and the Vorticists, of course, but had they heard, he asked—glancing up from the program with one of the booming laughs that became proverbial among his friends—of the *Spectrists*, the new poets who had just appeared in Pittsburgh; *they* were the ones to watch. Mr. Bynner, who had just come from Pittsburgh and who had been thinking what a good idea it would be to found a new school himself and to have some "fun with the extremists and with those of the critics who were over-anxious to be in the van," found himself, with this chance but inspired conversational gambit, faced with a virtual *fait accompli*. The possibilities of the words "spectral" or "spectric" flashed over him in a moment; and he remembered them when en route to Davenport the following day. He composed the first three poems on the train, and on arriving at Davenport, set forth to Arthur Davison Ficke and his wife his plan for a burlesque. Ficke, who was just as irritated as Mr. Bynner by the "schools" of the moment and who also thoroughly enjoyed a good joke, entered immediately into the spirit of the occasion. The Spectrists that evening came into being. (W. J. Smith 16–17)

The "good joke" was to last for two years, and to the surprise of Bynner and Ficke, the new "movement" was enormously successful virtually from its beginnings. In the fall of 1916, New York publisher Mitchell Kennerly published its anthology, *Spectra: A Book of Poetic Experiments*, which drove the reluctant authors "Morgan" and "Knish" into the limelight. On November 18, 1916, *The New Republic* announced: "There is a new school of poets, a new term to reckon with, a new theory to comprehend, a new manner to notice, a new humor to enjoy.

15

It is the Spectric school; composed, as far as the present publication goes, of a man, the cornerstone, and a woman, the keystone—Emanuel Morgan and Anne Knish" (W. J. Smith 5). Within months, the "new school" had been reviewed and debated by authors from Edgar Lee Masters to Amy Lowell, by publications as varied as *Poetry* magazine and the New York *Evening Sun*, which asked the public, "Are you hep to the Spectric Group?" The Spectrists made headlines in newspapers all over the country, rousing either fervent praise or condemnations from columnists in the Boston *Christian Register*, New York *Herald*, Detroit *News Tribune*, Los Angeles *Graphic*, Richmond *Journal*, Chicago *Evening Post*, Philadelphia *Public Register*. Literary journals too made haste to engage the Spectrists in their pages. "Knish" and "Morgan" had manuscripts accepted by *The Little Review* and *Poetry*, and *Others* assigned a special Spectric school issue for January 1917 (W. J. Smith 6).

The Spectrist manifesto, articulated by "Anne Knish" in the preface to the 1916 anthology, advocated a poetry of intensity, immediacy, vividness, and humor. "It is the aim of the Spectric group," wrote Knish, "to push the possibilities of poetic expression into a new region,—to attain a fresh brilliance of impression by a method not so wholly different from the methods of Futurist Painting" (W. J. Smith 3). The manifesto wavers between such seemingly serious statements and wildly equivocal claims such as: "The insubstantiality of the poet's spectres should touch with a tremulous vibrancy of ultimate fact the reader's sense of the immediate theme" (W. J. Smith 4). Similarly, Bynner's later accounts of the method of composition of Spectric poems ("The procedure was to let all reins go, to give the idea or the phrase complete head, to take whatever road or field or fence it chose. In other words it was a sort of runaway poetry, the poet seated in the wagon but the reins flung aside" [W. J. Smith 17–18]) took on in other instances a more serious tone of composition; Bynner later admitted that many of the wild Spectric methods had become quite serious stimuli for genuine poetic effort (W. J. Smith 43). What began as a joke, in short, developed a serious aesthetic undercurrent of experimentation tempered by humor and common sense.

Wallace Stevens entered the Spectrists' plans in their deliberations over whether to include this serious undertone in their manifesto. In the original draft of the preface to the anthology, the poets had intended to cite as an example of their school only one modern poet—Wallace Stevens—for whom both Ficke and Bynner had a high and genuine admiration. In a passage, omitted from the final draft as "too serious" for their enterprise, they wrote: "Among recent poets, apart from a small clan soon to be heard from, we have noted only one who can be regarded in any sure sense as a Spectrist. This one is Wallace Stevens. In his work appears a subtle but doubtless unconscious application of our method; and though a certain antiquation of touch prevents him from being fully classifiable as a Spectrist, it must be admitted that his work is by implication related to ours, a fact which we gladly acknowledge" (W. J. Smith 67). Not only, then, did Stevens elicit admiration from the avant-garde groups and movements, but even a distinctly anticoterie "movement," which explicitly valued more conservative poetic qualities of "beauty, vigor, and common sense," sought to include Stevens in its ranks, going so far as to jokingly chide the poet for an "antiquation of touch."

Although begun as a lighthearted protest and carried on as a two-year prank, the ramifications of the Spectra Hoax were felt long after it was dismantled. When the hoax was exposed in April 1918, critics, reviewers, and commentators who had applauded the movement found themselves caught with their evaluative guard down and retreated behind subtly more conservative editorial and critical policies. Others who had denounced the school not only commended their own caution but, in the case of naturally reactionary critics like Louis Untermeyer, used the hoax to justify their continued reticence about modernist authors, Stevens included. In addition, as Smith documents, a rash of minor hoaxes followed in the wake of Spectra, perpetuating the atmosphere of critical caution.

Set against all these incidental associations, which served to enrich and complicate Stevens' multifaceted image, there were two journals which provided the most sustained impact on Stevens' emergence and reception: Harriet Monroe's *Poetry* magazine in Chicago and the New York magazine-cum-movement *Others*, sponsored by Stevens' Village friends Walter Arensberg and Alfred Kreymborg. It was with Harriet Monroe that Stevens retained the closest personal and professional affiliation, publishing in her magazine from the time he was "discovered" in its 1914 War Issue until shortly before his death in 1955. Their correspondence during the teens and twenties was full of mutual encouragement, Stevens expressing support for the magazine and its policies and Monroe reciprocating with publication, circulation, and awards for Stevens' work. But the "growing pains" of *Poetry*, which attempted to offer a high-quality medium between the popular magazines and sporadic avant-garde reviews, at times touched on Stevens' career as well.

Three policies informed the conception and development of *Poetry* magazine. Monroe sought to provide the needed exposure and the even more needed financial support for the work of modern poets, with editorial standards based on "quality" and "neutrality." Moreover, the magazine was intended as a vehicle with which to further an "American Poetry Renaissance" to parallel the "Chicago Renaissance" in art and architecture which Monroe saw flourishing in the Midwest. Finally, Monroe was committed to the development of an American audience receptive to the new poetry and letters. Each of these policies, though noble, eventually led to difficulties for Monroe's enterprise.

In order to place Monroe's goals in perspective, we need to situate the magazine's beginnings in the context of the literary atmosphere of America in 1911, the year *Poetry* was conceived. Ellen Williams, in her detailed study *Harriet Monroe and the Poetry Renaissance*, describes the background against which *Poetry* emerged:

A good many American magazines in the first decade of the twentieth century . . . used poetry only as humbler papers used advertisements for patent medicines, as a convenient filler for the unused half or quarter column at the end of an article. This practice bred what came to be a recognized type, the "magazine poet" whose melodious trivia was standardized to fill a little space without distracting a reader.

. . . editors were perpetuating the weakness of American poetry. Manuscripts were being read by people who had no interest in or intelligence about poetry. American literary and cultural life had no structure. The literary world had no apparatus for finding poets, and did not know what to do with them when they somehow emerged into notice. (E. Williams 5–6)

Williams cites Ezra Pound's perception of the American literary scene to emphasize the constraints under which modern poets were operating in the early 1910s. In a letter to Harriet Monroe, Pound complains: "The reason why I abominate the American magazines and why I think they should be exterminated in revenge for the damage they have done American poetry is that they specialize in two or three tones. . . . There is no literature for precisely this reason, that they are all stuck into uniforms. They chase a popularity, express one or two moods, usually cheap complacency, or, elsewhere, stereotyped pity" (E. Williams 7).

Poetry was conceived as an alternative to the strictures of the commercial magazine market, which was neglecting poets of note in favor of "melodious trivia." In her advertising circular of 1912, announcing her prospectus for *Poetry,* Monroe cited her intent to offer poets "a chance to be heard in their own place, without the limitations imposed by the popular magazine." Monroe also offered "to print poems of greater length and of more intimate and serious character than the other magazines can afford to use." She made clear her editorial criteria of quality and neutrality, announcing: "All kinds of verse will be considered—narrative, dramatic, lyric— quality alone being the test of acceptance. . . . We shall read with special interest poems of modern significance, but the most classic subject will not be declined if it reaches a high standard of quality" (E. Williams 20). Finally, Monroe also vowed to "raise the rate paid for verse until it equals that paid for paintings, etchings, statuary, representing as much ability, time, and reputation" (E. Williams 21).

Monroe's belief—Williams describes it as a "mystical" certainty—was that with a favorable environment, the encouragement of space and pay, American poetry would experience an awakening that would rival the vitality of the artistic and architectural renaissance in "modern America" of the early 1910s. And she was not far wrong. Williams writes:

> The response to the circular was strong. William Rose Benet, Witter Bynner, Joseph Campbell, Bliss Carman, Arthur Davison Ficke, Wilfred Wilson Gibson, Alfred Percival Graves, Louis V. Ledoux, Vachel Lindsay, Amy Lowell, Percy MacKaye, Edwin Markham, Alice Meynell, Harold Monro, John G. Neihardt, Alfred Noyes, Ezra Pound, Cale Young Rice, John Hall Wheelock, Marguerite Wilkinson, and William Butler Yeats all sent in poems within six months of receiving it. By October,

1912, Harriet Monroe had enough material on hand that she could afford to be rigorous. *Poetry* was selective from the beginning. (E. Williams 22)

Ezra Pound's response to Harriet Monroe's advertisement established an influential, if tempestuous relationship between the two which was to see *Poetry* through its early years. In his letter dated August 18, 1912, Pound offered his services as "foreign correspondent" for the magazine, promising to keep Monroe "in touch with whatever is most dynamic in artistic thought, either here [London] or in Paris—as much of it as comes to me, and I *do* see nearly everyone that matters" (Pound, *Letters* 10). Initially, Pound was in agreement with Monroe's emphasis on quality and the "art" of poetry, and he was especially excited about the possibility of what he termed an "American Risorgimento." But although this enthusiasm made for an initially energetic working correspondence between the two, it was destined to sour within a few years, and eventually Pound made many bitter breaks with Monroe and *Poetry* magazine.

Monroe's third motive for the magazine was articulated in its motto, taken from Whitman: "To have great poets there must be great audiences too." Monroe's idea was to stimulate a fruitful relationship between the modern poet and the modern American audience; exposure was to be complemented by receptivity and support. During *Poetry*'s early years, however, Monroe's conception of this relationship wavered in its definition from the ideal of a democratic audience—Whitman's receptive "masses"—to that of a small number of intelligent readers. This issue caused battles between Pound and Monroe, whose heated correspondence became a formal debate in the editorial pages of the October 1914 issue. Pound's letter to Monroe dated January-February 1914 states his position regarding her goal: "You cling to one pernicious heresy. That of the need of an audience. Once and for all dammmm the audience. They eat us. We do not eat them" (E. Williams 95). Pound's contribution to the editorial "The Audience I" in the October issue goes on to denigrate the common audience in favor of the "few intelligent spirits" to whom the poet must look for support:

> It is true that the great artist has in the end, always, his audience, for the Lord of the universe sends into this world in each generation a few intelligent spirits, and these ultimately manage the rest. But this rest—this rabble, this multitude—does *not* create the great artist. They are aimless and drifting without him. They dare not inspect their own souls.
>
> It is true that the great artist has always a great audience, even in his life time; but it is not the *vulgo* but the spirits of irony and of destiny and of humor, sitting with him. (Pound, "Audience" 30)

Monroe's reply returns to Whitman to defend the need for the modern artist to speak to the people, to cultivate them as the audience through a poetry "based upon the whole life of his time, the common thought and feeling of the people" (Monroe, "Audience" 31). Yet only a few months earlier, at a literary party given by *Poetry* in March 1914, guest of honor William Butler Yeats delivered a speech on the poetic drama which in-

23

fluenced Monroe's later essays calling for a refined, almost aristocratic audience for the arts. Her essay reviewing the 1920 New York performance of Wallace Stevens' play *Three Travelers Watch a Sunrise* favorably and warmly paraphrased Yeats's description of "the aristocratic theatre in which from a dozen to fifty of the elect shall see plays worthy of spirits highly attuned and keyed, and shall pass them on authoritatively to the next age; a theatre modeled on the Noh drama of Japan, whose playwrights and players were always blissfully absorbed in their art and royally unconscious of the crowd" (Monroe, "Poetic Drama" 33). Monroe's changeable definitions of *audience* and *artist* and the relationship between the two continued in the editorial pages of *Poetry* for years.

But despite her faults, Harriet Monroe did provide the stable forum for modern poetry which was needed in the literary chaos of the time. And Wallace Stevens as contributor and personal correspondent was a recipient of Monroe's beneficence; *Poetry* published his work, praised it in critical reviews, awarded him prizes, and Monroe herself provided constructive criticism. In early letters to Stevens she steered him away from "Aubrey Beardsleyish" poems toward the mystical, powerful beauty of poems like "Sunday Morning." She received Stevens' first submission—the group "Phases" for the November 1914 issue—with delight, as she later recalled: "I was alone in the office when this group arrived almost too late for the War Number. I remember my eager reassembling of the page proofs to make room for two pages—all I could squeeze in—by this master of strange and beautiful rhythms" (E. Williams 113).

In a publication largely dominated in its early phases by Ezra Pound's suggestions and discoveries, Wallace Stevens was exclusively Harriet Monroe's, making for loyalty between Stevens and Monroe but eliciting a bristling hostility from the "Divine Ezra" toward Stevens. Not only did Pound conspicuously pan the November 1914 issue—an issue containing, besides Stevens' work, poetry and themes selected almost exclusively by Harriet Monroe—he virtually ignored every appearance of Wallace Stevens' work in *Poetry* between 1914 and 1921; it is a notable omission given Pound's constant and detailed critiques of Monroe's selections. But Pound showed similar antagonisms toward other poets she discovered, grumbling, for instance, over having to share *Poetry*'s pages with the poems of Vachel Lindsay: "He's all right, but we are not in the same movement or anything like it. I approve of his appearing in *Poetry* (so long as I am not supposed to want what he wants), but not in anything which I stand sponsor for as a healthy tendency" (Pound, *Letters* 55). Similarly, Pound affected condescension toward Carl Sandburg ("I don't think he's very important, but that's the sort of stuff we ought to print") and later renounced William Butler Yeats, at a time when Yeats continued to support Monroe's enterprise despite her quarrels with Pound.

Pound's coolness toward Stevens continued for years; his critique of Stevens' appearance in the "American number" of *The Little Review*, June 1918, almost vengefully disparages American art in comparison to European and dismisses poets who are not members of his own camp:

> What a disparity! Endlessness of Hecht's desolate adjectives, the sillyness of Kreymborg, Amy Lowell the female poet, the endeavors of Williams to create a stir, the Rollo Peters stage scenery of Wallace Stevens. . . . But give us more of Lewis, Lewis, Wyndham Lewis, and Eliot! And what happened to Jessie Dismorr?
>
> T. S. Eliot makes a writer like Stevens look like a schoolgirl straining for originality.
>
> Wallace Stevens' group has charm, but is somewhat romantic. I mean the charm is due to a romantic sort of exaggeration. It is not unlike the Georgian Anthology; though modernized. Or, it is tired Chinese—if that has any meaning to you—which the mood cannot condone. (E. Williams 222–23)

Critic Marjorie Perloff quotes Pound, as late as 1955 responding haughtily to William Carlos Williams' request for comment on the obituary essay Williams had just written for Stevens:

> As to yr/ pal/ Wally S/ . . it wd/ be highly improper for me to have opinions of yr/ opinion of a bloke I haven't read
>
> and DOUBT like all hell
> that yu will be able to PURR-suade me to venture on
> with such a
> hellUVAlot I don't know and WANT to find out (Perloff 485)

In the years of his emergence, though, not only did Stevens suffer the indifference of Pound, whose voice was so influential in avant-garde circles, he was also included by proxy in attacks on *Poetry* by conservative critics who questioned Harriet Monroe's aims. The earliest critical mention of Stevens' work was in the context of a bitter attack on *Poetry,* an article titled "Chicago Poets and Poetry" in the Feburary 1916 issue of *Minaret.* The review, signed simply "The Editor," excoriates *Poetry* magazine and its poets: "In order to prove how worthless and perverted is the work appearing in this publication, I need only quote examples from the contents of the twelve numbers during the year 1914" ("Chicago Poets" 24). The article snipes at poems by Lindsay and Sandburg, draws up a list of "insignificants" which include Ezra Pound and H.D., and finally takes up the fated War Number in which Stevens' first poems appeared. "If anyone can suggest to me a magazine that has had worse poems through its whole existence, than this individual War Number had, I would like to see the magazine," writes this reviewer, using passages from Stevens' "Phases" to illustrate poetry "untruthful, and nauseating to read" and concluding, "I do not care to stain the pages of this magazine with such drivel" ("Chicago Poets" 24–25). Indeed, it was an inauspicious beginning for Stevens' verse, drawn into the wider battle over *Poetry* and modern art itself, a war which raged for a number of years in the pages of establishment journals like *The Dial* and in the savage attacks of such critics as Edgar Jepson in the *English Review,* who, as Williams summarizes, condemned Harriet Monroe's collection of "maundering dribble" from "ploppeyed bungaroos" and "gawky cowboys in the art" (E. Williams 234).

Monroe's attempts to mediate between old-school conservatism and the rash inflammability of the avant-garde by advocating fairness and neutrality sadly seemed to please neither side. Established institutions condemned her openness to new art, and modern artists themselves resented what they saw as her unselective eclecticism and the "safety" of her editorial policies. By mid-decade, *Poetry* having broken significant ground for the advent of other small literary magazines, a number of reviews were established in direct competition with *Poetry,* the most vocal of which seems to have been *Others.*

Alfred Kreymborg in his third-person autobiography recounts his meeting with Walter Conrad Arensberg in 1915, during which the idea of *Others* was conceived to fill a gap between the fickle emergence of a review like *Rogue* and the "unselectivity" of the more solidly established *Poetry* magazine. Kreymborg, here using his nickname "Krimmie," writes:

> Arensberg was passionately fond of Pound and the Imagists, asked many pertinent questions about the Imagist issue in The Glebe [an earlier literary undertaking of Kreymborg's], confided that Rogue would never do, couldn't last in any event, and what was needed in America was a poetry magazine, not like Poetry in Chicago, which admitted too many compromises, but a paper dedicating its energies to experiment throughout. . . . Krimmie promised to get in touch once more with Pound and other poets he knew, and to consult a printer he had recently met who called himself Mr. Liberty. They had decided on a magazine limited to sixteen pages and five hundred copies per issue. "We'll have Wallace Stevens and Mina Loy to begin with," Walter de-

28

clared. "They alone," Krimmie interrupted, "would create the paper we have in mind." "So would you," Walter added; "so would you," responded Krimmie. (Kreymborg, *Troubadour* 221)

The first issue came out in July 1915, announcing the motto "The old expressions are with us always, and there are always others."

Kreymborg claimed that "Others was merely to print the work of men and women who were trying themselves in new forms. A principle of rigid privacy was determined upon. There was to be in no sense of the word a group" (Kreymborg, *Troubadour* 222). Still, the controversial nature of its first three issues drew quite a bit of attention, and it was not long before the *Others* poets became recognized as a movement of their own. Beyond the opening issues—which contained an impressive collection of poems by Mina Loy, Orrick Johns, Amy Lowell, William Carlos Williams, Skipwith Cannel, as well as Stevens' "Peter Quince at the Clavier" and T. S. Eliot's "Portrait of a Lady"—within four years the *Others* group had issued three anthologies, two published by Alfred Knopf in 1916 and 1917 and a third in 1918 by Nicholas L. Brown. This kind of publicity, coupled with the growing repute of individual *Others* poets—Pound, Eliot, Marianne Moore, Stevens, Williams, and minor authors Orrick Johns, Maxwell Bodenheim, and Mina Loy—insured the national notice this small movement received.

Even Kreymborg eventually acknowledged the community of *Others*, calling it a "new league" of poets committed to a basis of experimentation, who outdistanced the imagists and their concentration merely on image by experimenting with all aspects of poetic technique—rhythm, form, and language. Kreymborg, then living in Grantwood, New Jersey, began a Sunday ritual gathering of the *Others* artists—a form of bonding which Harriet Monroe lacked—to "talk shop" and exchange manuscripts and ideas. Stevens declined invitations to Grantwood, but when Kreymborg moved back to the city, he, too, began to frequent the poetic group whose "editorial room was the kitchen" of Kreymborg's New York apartment, "and the icebox was its center" (Hoffman, Allen, Ulrich 48).

For the critics, too, *Others* was a distinct entity—an "easy tag"—although each seemed to attach his or her own idiosyncratic connotations to the label. For Louis Untermeyer, the *Others* poets stood for the "aesthetic" school, represented by Pound, Eliot, Stevens, and their antihumanistic verse (Untermeyer, "Ivory Tower" 60–61). Other critics used the journal title as a pseudonym for Kreymborg—himself a wildly erratic poet—and so as a synonym for unbounded, radical experimentation. Kreymborg reports that early reactions to the *Others* group amounted to "travesties, ballyragging, every conceivable form of ridicule," giving *Others* "a reputation bordering on infamy" (Kreymborg, *Troubadour* 235). Harriet Monroe, too, had her own reasons for wanting the *Others* poets defined as "the people who were too youthful or too radical to get into *Poetry*," for she rightly felt the competition from Kreymborg's periodical, which was not only getting significant, if negative attention but was also siphoning off contributors from *Poetry*'s ranks (E. Williams 150).

Although *Others* could not maintain its impressive beginnings, for some reason the magazine took years to follow the fate of other small, radical reviews. Kreymborg recalls:

> Toward the tail-end, when Krimmie was positive the venture had outlived its usefulness, Lola [Ridge] managed to keep it going a while. Williams, who had soured on the movement to a degree that caused him to pounce on an issue he edited with a grieving, ranting, coroner's inquest he called Belly Music, assured his readers, "Others is dead," and promised to bury it with the present issue. The *post-mortem* on the part of Lola, with her happy mania for appearing among moribund things and reviving them, puzzled the subscribers. Here was still another number on top of the one they had been asked to accept as an obituary. How many times was the thing to die and bob up again? (Kreymborg, *Troubadour* 330)

In fact, the *Others* group continued even after the decease of the magazine, meeting, according to Frederick J. Hoffman, Charles Allen, and Carolyn F. Ulrich, in the apartment of Lola Ridge: "It was during one of these meetings that Scofield Thayer, who had recently become co-publisher and co-editor of *The Dial*, met many of the people whose work he was soon to begin printing. *The Dial*'s poetic tone was really a continuation of the *Others* spirit, even before Marianne Moore became *The Dial* editor in 1925" (Hoffman, Allen, Ulrich 51).

Wallace Stevens and the Critical Schools

By the 1920s, Scofield Thayer's more liberal editorship of *The Dial,* along with the fact that many of the once-new poets had become established, caused a new shift in patterns of publication, with poets like Pound, Moore, Williams, Eliot, and Stevens not only accepted but even courted by larger "commercial" magazines such as *The Dial* and *The New Republic.* These periodicals, once so quick to condemn the modernist movement in poetry, now accepted as good business the spirit of the experimental and the new in art. And although Stevens continued to publish in smaller, anti-commercial magazines such as *Broom, Secession, The Modern School,* and *The Little Review,* by the early 1920s his "emergence" was complete. With the long-awaited publication of *Harmonium* in 1923, Stevens—still trailing a confusing background of affiliations with dandies, rogues, aesthetes, dadaists, imagists, symbolists, exquisites, and *Others*—became a serious subject for the critics.

2

Concepts of Irony in Stevens' Early Critics

Scarcely ever is his attack a direct and simple one. Generally, it is oblique, patronizing and twisted with self-intended mockery. The measure is sometimes languid, sometimes mincing, almost invariably buffoon-like. It tips, pirouettes, executes an hundred little foppish turns and graces. It rocks complacently like a preening waterfowl upon its perch; waltzes in grotesque fury; keens like a comic rabbi; begins a movement and lets it end in air. . . . The poet is perceived leaning in evident boredom against the corner of a mantlepiece, or adjusting his monocle with a look of martyrdom.

—Paul Rosenfeld, *Men Seen: Twenty-Four Modern Authors*

Stevens' early reception among the critics was a confused, often controversial affair—and in this way resembled much of the general hesitation and ambivalence toward the "new poetry" of the 1910s and 1920s. We can attempt to explain the somewhat reluctant critical acceptance of Stevens by pointing to Pound's silence about Stevens' work, to the often dubious and radical reputation of Kreymborg and the *Others* group which adhered to Stevens, or to the general backlash of the Spectra and subsequent literary hoaxes, which may have created a subtly more conservative critical environment for the work of modern artists. But beyond the issues of Stevens' publication, circulation, and literary affiliations, the fact remains that new and experimental movements in poetry were creating a correlative upheaval in criticism. It was a time for the questioning and readjustment of general aesthetic standards in response to a new poetry which resisted traditional interpretation.

33

A number of scholars see early Stevens criticism as an attempt to "define Stevens's style, to place him in a tradition" (Ehrenpreis 37); they interpret the controversy over Stevens' acceptance in the 1910s and 1920s as a question of French versus American aesthetics, or what Abbie Willard calls "the issue of Stevens's literary heritage" (Willard 54). This would be an ideal theory if it could be substantiated in the criticism itself, but as a viable pattern to early Stevens criticism the European/American debate remains secondary. Irvin Ehrenpreis names René Taupin, Alfred Kreymborg, and John Gould Fletcher as indicators of Stevens' "French" background; however, these critics' statements are ambivalent at best.

Taupin's study of symbolism, *L'Influence du symbolisme français sur la poésie américaine* (1929), mentions Wallace Stevens as a poet who "knew French poetry. He even translated French poems; but," Taupin writes, "*he never imitated them directly*" (Taupin 235, italics mine). Taupin does point out that the spirit of the French language—the "elegance and nuance" of vocabulary, the use of exclamatory and interrogative sentence structures, and the "subtleties of expression" of the French style—can be seen in Stevens' verse, but he agrees with Gorham Munson that Stevens is "distinctly American" in temperament (Taupin 237). In all, Taupin seems more to adulate a refinement of language he attributes to the French than to truly attempt to place Stevens in a fixed heritage.

In a similar way, critics like John Gould Fletcher were spanning the question of Stevens' literary characteristics with such ambiguous statements as "He carefully dresses his verses in the latest French mode. Only the vague sense of disquiet, pulsing underneath, proves him to be essentially American" (Fletcher, Review 28). Compare Alfred Kreymborg's portrait of Stevens as "neither a misanthrope nor a snob, but one of the wisest and subtlest of natives: an American reared on French Symbolism, on the philosophic poetry of the aristocratic Jules Laforgue. Not to mention an older race: the aristocratic Elizabethans" (Kreymborg, *Strength* 501). Again, Kreymborg's crediting of Stevens with international, panhistoric qualities seems more a general compliment to the poet than a true search for literary lineage.

In the works of other critics—Conrad Aiken and Louis Untermeyer, for example—the question of French versus American traits was quite evidently subsumed under more encompassing issues of poetic theory. Aiken and Untermeyer were the first to bring Stevens into the critical fray, in a skirmish in the pages of *The New Republic,* May 10, 1919. Their articles, titled respectively "The Ivory Tower I" and "The Ivory Tower II," reflect the two essential—and essentially antagonistic—ideologies in early twentieth-century American criticism which battled over Stevens' inclusion in the canon.

Willard attempts to paraphrase the Aiken-Untermeyer debate: "Is [Stevens] part of the 'lustihood' and 'democracy' of Americanism or to be associated with the magical and elaborated art for art's sake of French Impressionism?" (Willard 54). This summary, however, provides too narrow a frame for their controversy. Although Untermeyer does attempt to create a hierarchy of "American" authors, it is a group from which Stevens is notably absent. Conversely, nowhere does Aiken attempt to associate Stevens with any foreign or domestic influence. In fact, he questions the very suppositions inherent in tracing literary lineage, the classification of authors and works into schools which deny their complexity and individuality. "[It] is not a question of American as against European," writes Aiken in his 1919 collection *Scepticisms*, in which "The Ivory Tower" was the last essay; "it is simply and solely a question of whether the given poem has beauty, subtlety, intensity, and depth, or whether it has not, and in what degree" (Aiken, *Scepticisms* 295). The question here is one of standards, of general ideologies, rather than the facile labeling of Stevens as participator in fashionable Continental trends. As Untermeyer himself claims, the debate encompasses "the direct impact of two opposed theories . . . the aesthetic policy in art and the humanist approach toward it" (Untermeyer, "Ivory Tower" 60).

Aiken's essay questions Untermeyer's "acrimonious antipathies" toward Stevens and other poets: Pound and the imagists, Eliot, Bodenheim, Kreymborg and the *Others*. He opens his attack on Untermeyer's collection *The New Era in American Poetry* with a short dissertation on the implicated nature of the poet-critic, who, by Aiken's own confession, is "vitally concerned with the success or failure of this or that particular strain of work" (Aiken, "Ivory Tower" 58). The benefits of "warmth" and "intensity" in criticism resulting from this unavoidable bias are balanced by the drawback of "unreliability" in matters requiring critical objectivity. Although Aiken concedes that "this unreliability will be diminished . . . in the degree in which the critic is aware of his bias and makes allowance for it," he feels that Untermeyer has neglected this primary step of self-awareness—we might almost say hermeneutical awareness—and failed to recognize his own bias, not only as a poet but as an essentially reactionary poet in an era "destined for rapid changes" (Aiken, "Ivory Tower" 58).

Untermeyer's critical policy, as articulated in this review, propounds a combination of "Americanism, lustihood, glorification of reality (facing of the world of fact) democracy" (Aiken, "Ivory Tower" 59) as standards in judging poetry—premises which can be traced to Untermeyer's new humanistic belief in art as "community expression." According to Aiken's sardonic paraphrase: "Away, therefore, with the pernicious doctrine of 'art for art's sake'; and down with the ivory tower. Art has a human function to perform" (Aiken, "Ivory Tower" 59). For Untermeyer, art must bear a "message," reflect social consciousness in general and in paticular demonstrate a type of nationalism which portrays American art as vigorous, passionate, enthusiastic, straightforward.

For Aiken, however, these premises reveal a critical "shortsightedness and essential viciousness" resting on ultimately unsound metaphysical, sociological, and nationalistic foundations. More concretely, he believes they have led Untermeyer to miss the "finer note" in modern American poetry and to erect as a result a ludicrous literary canon which "has cast into undue prominence the work of Oppenheim, Giovannitti, Charles Erskine Scott Wood, Alter Brody; it has put a wrong emphasis on the work of Sandburg; and, per contra, it has thrown into a shadow by no means deserved the work of such poets as do not, in Mr. Untermeyer's opinion, fulfil their social contracts,—such poets as T. S. Eliot, John Gould Fletcher, Wallace Stevens, Maxwell Bodenheim, the Imagists, and the entire strain in poetry for which they inconspicuously stand" (Aiken, "Ivory Tower" 59).

As might be expected, Aiken challenges Untermeyer's neglect of aesthetic principles in favor of sociological considerations and the consequent judging of art as limited communal expression: "Are we to conclude from these premises that art is any the less art because it fails to satisfy a contemporary hunger for this or that social change? Are we to conclude that art is any the more richly art because it bears conspicuously and consciously the label 'Made in America'?" (Aiken, "Ivory Tower" 59). Social and national concerns, furthermore, are "local and temporary: they change like the fashions. . . . the odds are great that what is a burning issue today will be a familiar fact, and the occasion of a yawn, tomorrow" (Aiken, "Ivory Tower" 59).

Instead, Aiken advocates the "absolute poetry" of Stevens, Eliot, Kreymborg, and the *Others* group, a poetry which "delivers no message, is imbued with no doctrine, a poetry which exists only for the sake of magic,—magic of beauty on the one hand, magic of reality on the other, but both struck at rather through a play of implication than through matter-of-fact statement. . . . It is the be-all and end-all of such poetry that it should be a perfectly formed and felt work of art: and the greater the elaboration and subtlety consistent with such perfection the more inexhaustible will it be, the longer it will endure" (Aiken, "Ivory Tower" 60). "Art is art," Aiken concludes, "not sociology, not philosophy."

Some critics have seen nothing but the *art-pour-l'art* stance in Aiken's theory, but a close reading of Aiken's rhetoric reveals a deeper level of ideology—an ideology in which art *is* sociology, *is* philosophy, is in fact a penetration of human and ontological reality of an alternative but equally salient kind. In comparing Whitman to Poe as examples, respectively, of theories of art as social consciousness and art for art's sake, Aiken questions whether Poe's tendency does not reflect just as valid a communal concern and human "hunger" as Whitman's: "Is such an art as Poe's, which as well as any illustrates the virtues and defects of the theory of art for art's sake, a whit the less a form of community expression, a whit the less satisfying to the human hunger for articulation, than such an art as Mr. Untermeyer seems to favor?" Aiken contends that the poems of Eliot, Fletcher, Stevens, and company "are clearly finer, and more universal in appeal, than anything as yet given us by Oppenheim, Giovannitti, Wood, or Brody" (Aiken, "Ivory Tower" 59).

Clearly, Aiken finds his "absolute" poets more articulate than Untermeyer's group, but he also goes on to question the integrity of Untermeyer's poets as "deliverers of the 'message.'" The "message" they bear—and, implicitly, their inclusion in Untermeyer's collection because it is the message he wants to hear—he considers a "primitively naive" statement of unquestioned affirmation and faith. It is a poetry, for Aiken, of "the unflinchingly masculine, the explicitly affirmative (what

Nietzsche termed the 'yea-saying'), the triumphantly and not too reflectively acceptant; the vigorous, in short, rather than the cerebral or oblique or disillusioned, the enthusiastic and downright or sanely sentimental rather than the interpretative or analytic or psychologically tenuous" (Aiken, "Ivory Tower" 59).

The "affirmative" against the "disillusioned," the "acceptant" against the "analytic," the "sanely sentimental" against the exploratively "tenuous" mind—in short, the superficial and mystified against the ironic mentality is the issue at play here. It is here that we find the crux of Aiken's ideology, of the early critical attitude receptive to the perplexities of language and the mental rigor of a poetry like Wallace Stevens'. Underlying this criticism is a basic weltanschauung based on ironically seeing through accepted order to relativity, chaos, flux, and disillusion. For Aiken and others this was an attitude psychologically and ontologically more "real" than Untermeyer's wishfully censored "word of fact." It is this concept of seeing through traditional stabilities of religion, society, human nature, even the referentiality of language which runs as a theme through most early criticism of Stevens' work.

As a keystone to early Stevens criticism, the concept of irony and its varied manifestations was informed by a reassessment of reality and a subsequent emphasis on the realism of relative, individual expression. Three major areas of controversy over Stevens' poetry were the question of "meaning," the use of language, and the artist's persona within the poetry. More specifically, the underlying debate came to center upon an ironical world

40

view, linguistic irony, and the character of the ironist in modern life and letters.

Aiken's attack on Untermeyer introduced this concept of differing world views. Aiken's receptivity to Stevens, Pound, Eliot, and other modernists reflected his appreciation of their greater rigor of thought, complexity of expression, and skepticism toward nostalgic attitudes of affirmation handed down from the past. Untermeyer's rebuttal, on the other hand, is replete with praise for poetry's "unconquerable affirmation," its "faith" and "confidence of soul," and the poet's "striving to confirm some sort of God." For Untermeyer "the artist is more of a child; illusion buoys him up; a naive assurance sweeps him on. A belief in the beauty and immortality of life, a belief so neatly scorned by Mr. Aiken, possesses him and is at the heart of his fullest achievement. No major art has ever existed and, with a few brilliant exceptions, no art-work has survived that has not been built on faith" (Untermeyer, "Ivory Tower" 61). Untermeyer's stress on "spirituality" and "moral passion" brings him close to the neo-Augustan tenets of new humanism calling for universal norms and values as the test of art. Untermeyer claims for art the duty of "glorified communication, a sharing of life," and the "mere verbal legerdemain of the Pound-Stevens-Arensberg-Others" group falls far short of such ends. Even stylistically, Untermeyer denounces this group for unreadability, insisting that "the great workers are simple and direct, 'never,' as Whitman said, 'secret or obscure'" (Untermeyer, "Ivory Tower" 61).

But secrecy and obscurity became, for critics operating under other standards, a favorable aspect of Stevens' work. Llewelyn Powys, for example, saw Stevens' obscurity as a mimetic technique reflective of the nature of the world itself:

> And it may well be that [Stevens'] eccentric verse does actually reveal more of the insecure fluctuating secrets of the universe than are to be found in other more sedate, more decorous artistic creations. Wavering, uncertain, bereft of ancient consolations, the human race comes more and more to realize that it has won to consciousness in a world in which all is relative and undulating. . . .
>
> From king to beggar we are aware of our manifold delusions, aware that nothing is as false as the face value of things. We have, alas! grown only too cognizant of the essential mendacity of the physical aspects of a universe that has no bottom. And this being so, it is perhaps in suggestions, in mere phantasms, that we come nearest to the evocations of that fourth-dimensional consciousness which may well be furthest removed from illusion. If the surface of the visible world then is nothing, who can tell but that the shadows of the surface of the visible world may be everything? And no poet, not Baudelaire, not Edgar Allan Poe even, has revealed with a surer touch, a surer ambiguity, the very shades and tinctures of this indefinable borderland than has this ultramodern supersubtle lawyer from the confines of Hartford, Connecticut. (Powys 45)

Another critical advocate of Stevens' "sure ambiguity" and his reflection of the "bottomless universe" was *Poetry* magazine's editorial assistant and critic Marjorie Allen Seiffert. In a 1923 review she too casts Stevens in the light of consummate re-presenter of the fluctuating cosmos. "Mr. Stevens doesn't mean to be any more illuminating than life itself," announces this review redolent with images of irony and the penetration of illusion to achieve the "substratum of reality." In Stevens' poetry, as in life, "accustomed realities are concealed"; here "emotion lurks behind design," and "we must peer through" to glimpse a reality which "flits into obscurity" (Seiffert 155, 160). John Gould Fletcher as well, in an essay published that year, echoes Seiffert and Powys' defense of Stevensian evanescence. The poet's "obscurity comes from a wealth of meaning and allusion which are unavoidable," writes Fletcher; Stevens remains preoccupied with "something more important than externals" (Fletcher, "Revival" 356).

But it is Maxwell Bodenheim who perhaps articulates most fully the ironic Stevensian world view, the casting off of accepted stabilities and standards. For Bodenheim poets exhibit a mentality "in which forms, colors, and substances take on their actual shapes and throw off the distortions, false grandeurs, and sleekly emotional lies which men have fastened upon them" (Bodenheim 96). Stevens' bringing forth of his subjects into reality out of "that unreality concocted by man to soothe his baffled life" Bodenheim considers a valuable characteristic of the new poetry:

> The old emotional eloquence, dramatic ecstasies of phraseology, and suave oratory with which most poets have always addressed birds, trees, flowers, and the lives of men, is disappearing, and in its place there has been born a struggle on the part of the poet to wrestle with

the concrete forms about him. . . . This battle, in which wood becomes wood and stone becomes stone and the poet sees the wood and stone that lie within himself and breaks them into articulate variations—this battle is not a new one. . . . It is the abstracted, impersonal glare of eyes that do not seek to judge, praise, or blame, but are immersed in patiently subtracting and multiplying the bare words, expressions, forms, and colors of life, in order to arrive at the nearest possible approach to the sum total of their essence. (Bodenheim 97)

Bodenheim's view of this new type of phenomenology, this "attempt to unearth an inner reality which often conflicts with the surface plausibility and visual falseness which men have ever called 'reality,'" not surprisingly lauds Wallace Stevens as a major modern voice (Bodenheim 97).

It was not only Stevens' implicit ideology but his use of the medium which alarmed and perplexed yet another contingent of critics. An anonymous 1923 review in *Bookman*, referring to Stevens' "gay diablerie in arranging grotesque word patterns which seem quite liberated from time and space and prosody and all the other ills to which the flesh is heir" (*Bookman* 483), echoes, tongue-in-cheek, the more vituperative objections to Stevens' calculated irreverence for the univalence and referentiality of language. Stevens' gorgeous, exotic vocabulary and syntax displeased critics bent on preserving the communicative clarity of Louis Untermeyer's "simple and direct" standard for poetic diction. As late as 1936 John Holmes could write of Stevens that he was "one of the most successful non-communicating poets of his day"

(Holmes 294), and in the critical controversy over Stevens during the 1910s and 1920s his use of language was a persistent issue.

Louis Untermeyer was at the helm of opposition to Stevens' play with the traditional stabilities of language, charging him with a "determined obscurity" and an "uncertainty of communication . . . which lead one to doubt whether its author even cares to communicate in a tongue familiar to the reader" (Untermeyer, "Five Poets" 159). Other critics retreated behind either mild ridicule or dismissal, but virtually no early review of Stevens fails to note the difficulties of his language. Laura Riding and Robert Graves, in their 1927 overview, *A Survey of Modernist Poetry*, examine this reaction against innovative uses of language as a way of protecting the safety of the "accepted code" of speech. Modernist literature, in its attempt to freshen clichés of language and thought, often disturbed those with a more conservative, social, proprietary stand toward language. For Riding and Graves, however, a renewed contact with language in poetry runs parallel to a renewed contact with the universe, thought, reality—an enterprise needed in an age of "safe" and stereotyped thought. They examine a reviewer's antagonism toward what he sees as alienating, antisocial uses of language in modernist poetry. Quoted in *A Survey*, the anonymous reviewer writes, "It is as if [modernist poetry's] object were to express that element only in the poet's nature by virtue of which he feels himself an alien in the universe, or at least an alien from what he takes to be the universe acknowledged by the rest of mankind." Riding and Graves respond:

45

But the truth is that "the rest of mankind" is for the most part totally unaware of the universe and constantly depends on the poet to give it a secondhand sense of the universe through language. Because this language has been accepted ready-made by "the rest of mankind" without understanding the reasons for it, it becomes, by "progress," stereotyped and loses its meaning; and the poet is called upon again to remind people what the universe really looks and feels like, that is, what language means. If he does this conscientiously he must use language in a fresh way or even . . . invent new language. But, if he does, he will be certain to antagonize for a while those who keep asking poetry to do their more difficult thinking for them. (Riding and Graves 94–95)

New language for a new perspective, for contact with a new "reality," became a characteristic of the new poetry, accompanied by the poets' demand for more rigorous and original thought. Discovering the richness of language demanded a shattering of language's accepted social uses, the surface order of a univalent public speech. Raymond Holden was another early critic who recognized Stevens' penetration of the assumed stability of language as an exploration of the multidimensionality of words:

Mr. Stevens, either consciously or unconsciously, believes that words uttered or written may have a value separate from their meaning in terms of human speech. When it is considered that *yaitzo* and egg, very different sounds indeed, have exactly the same meaning, the one in Russian and the other in English, it may be agreed that the actual significance of sound cannot universally

46

be in its use in any given language. It is not, therefore, stretching the point to any dangerous degree, to say that there is, in syllables written and pronounced, a sense value differing from, if not entirely independent of, their meaning to the literate mind. After all it is the illiterate portion of the mind which covets the subtler music of the world. I feel that Mr. Stevens has addressed himself to this covetousness with conspicuous success. (Holden 17)

Whether viewing it as a violation or a liberation, a deliberate obscuring of sense or an ironic seeing through to new senses, nearly every critic needed to address the novelty of vocabulary and the perplexing blend of simplicity with gorgeous, tangled language in Stevens' poetry. Analyses of the function and significance of poetic language reveal much about critical assumptions—from a denigration of the poet's breach of normal communicative standards to praise for Stevens' sensuous musical skill with language as nonreferential medium, to attempts to define innovative language as a heightened contact with the universe or the self. Stevens' use of language even took on nationalistic significance for a critic like Harriet Monroe, whose essay "The Free Verse Movement in America" (1924) addresses the problems and strictures for American poets working with a language inherited from England which entails "inherited racial traditions and loyalties, inherited literary forms and practices. It means acceptance instead of creation, acquiescence instead of a fresh adventure" (Monroe, "Free Verse" 691). For Monroe, experiments in language and sound such as those employed by Stevens suggested a breaking of conventions and a move into a new, individual poetry.

The ironic use of language represented an exploration and discovery of new levels beyond the standard sense of language, much as the ironic weltanschauung of Stevens and other modernists represented a seeing through to a more fluid and complex sense of reality. Yet we must distinguish the concept of irony as the "message" of a certain world order (or lack thereof) from the sense of irony as attitude, or posture, in the poetic persona. Where the ironic world view pointed out a perplexing cosmos, a "bottomless" twentieth-century universe, the ironic attitude stood as a reaction to that apprehension of flux and relativity. Stevens' stance as ironist is one which critics have continually tried to identify and either praise or dismiss. Much early criticism explores the ironic persona in Stevens' poetry, dubbing him Pierrot, humorist, urbane intellectual, agonized clown, dandy, Augustan wit, cynic, spectator, cerebralist—among other labels which serve either to commend or indict the poet. One of the major early objections to Stevens was his supposedly "inhuman" voice—Stevens as pure, icy intellectual without emotions, without the requisite "humanity"—a characteristic which others variously attempt to commend, explain, or deny.

An interesting analysis of the modernist poetic attitude is again provided by Riding and Graves. The authors identify the "Lost Generation" and its sense of gloom, which they consider different from two previous manifestations of "gloom" in literary history: the Byronic and the "decadence" of the 1890s. For the modern

48

generation, the loss of ideas presents less a sense of crisis and despair than a type of "sophistication" and maturity of vision, breeding a correspondent cynicism and "common sense" in the approach to life, reality, and art. Even this common sense, however, differs from its traditional definition in being "not of the substance of happy platitudes but of hard wit" (Riding and Graves 225). The modernists are a generation without sentimentality and, so, without pessimism, since, according to Riding and Graves, "pessimism is sentimental." Instead, this generation announces "a drastic alteration in traditional values; but without the violence characteristic of minds that have reached this stage by more emotional paths. . . . It must not only revise traditional values; it must appreciate new ones" (Riding and Graves 226–27).

For Riding and Graves, the new poetry's penetrating, ironic vision is marked by certain characteristics and devices which must be understood in order to understand the poetry. Self-mockery becomes an important element in a poetry which recognizes the dilemma of art in the modern age—a Crispin-like "formal clownishness" which nonetheless demonstrates the need as well as the futility of creation. The burlesque of the modern artist, furthermore, is "pure burlesque," a "tearless, heartless" clowning divorced from a sense of audience. The humor is subtle, aristocratic, rarefied to the point where it excludes a common audience, and in precisely this exclusion it creates a vehicle with which to conduct its "bright game of spite against the middle-classes," its "jokes . . . against modern civilization" (Riding and Graves 247, 242).

But the modern artist is not only engaged in a game of sniping and destruction. The poet also evinces a revitalizing neutrality toward poetic subjects that have become exhausted through spiritual "elevation," moving toward new subjects and styles which refresh poetry, toward a play with language which renews the energy of the medium and demonstrates the "Protean powers" of poetry and the imagination (Riding and Graves 243). Riding and Graves conclude their chapter with a description of the paradoxical position of the modernist poet, an equipoise of humor and seriousness, an infinity mirror of double irony: "He completes and in a sense contradicts his clownishness by revealing that even clownishness is a joke: that it is a joke to be writing poetry, a joke to be writing modernist poetry. By this token he belongs to the most serious generation of poets that has ever written; with the final self-protective corollary, of course, that it is also a joke to be serious" (Riding and Graves 251–52).

The complex irony-within-irony of modernist poetry and the poet's attitude toward reality, art, and the artist's own situation foreshadow many of the problems which more traditional critics encountered in assessing Stevens, distinctly a poet of this self-conscious, humorous-serious, ironic generation. Gorham Munson, for instance, attempts to accommodate Stevens' disturbing irony in terms of the antiquated figure of the dandy. Munson finds in Stevens a demonstration that "life as a spectacle is disturbing and horrifying as well as interesting and delightful: it is inevitably tossed by the 'torments of confusion' and the dandy, to preserve his values, to maintain his urbane order and demeanor, must perforce adopt protective measures" (Munson 82). For Munson, it is a system of personal self-defense which informs Stevens' verse: "The safeguards that Stevens employs to keep 'the torments of confusion' from rumpling his attitude are three: wit, speculation, and reticence" (Munson 82). In the face of the disturbing nature of the universe, Stevens' art becomes "a minute but sustained harmony floating above the chaos of life. It is whole and understandable and therefore a refuge in a life that is too fragmentary and perplexing. It, being form, is a polite answer to the hugeness which we cannot form" (Munson 84).

Harriet Monroe also recognizes the "malaise of our time, its bitter suffering, its conviction of futility," yet also sees Stevens as an ironist of a politer vein, one of "the race of the great humorists" rather than the craftsman of "agonized irony" she saw in T. S. Eliot (Monroe, "Cavalier" 324). She not surprisingly commends Stevens' greater civility, his lighter touch in confronting an age of crisis. Marjorie Allen Seiffert continues the *Poetry* standard in complimenting Stevens as light, urbane ironist. "One has had so much of the heavy poets," she writes, "that it is sheer delight to find one who handles his matter without the *grand serieux*" (Seiffert 158).

But while Stevens was being sketched as the disinterested humorist and dandy by the subtle conservatism evident in such journals as *Poetry* or in Munson's brand of new humanism, Paul Rosenfeld saw another, bleaker strain in Stevens' ironic attitude. Rosenfeld dwells on the futility at the heart of Stevens' verse. Stevens, for him, is a Pierrot "of a distinct Laforguian cut," whose verse turns "melancholy soliloquy" into "a silvery music signifying nothing . . . a bland, curiously philosophical movement of the soul without signification" (Rosenfeld 157–59). Rosenfeld's extensive character sketch of Stevens as Pierrot portrays the modern artist caught in an aggressive internal struggle:

> Uncomfortably self-aware, the pitiable gentleman can never quite spend himself in living, and remains emotionally naive, O Horrors! as a romantic poet. To be sure, little in his mask betrays him. Pierrot is sophisticated, worldly, lettered, read in philosophical authors Greek and Germanic. He is excessively correct, partly from natural elegance and partly in protest against romantic dishevelment; and functions suavely as reader to an empress, teller of a London bank, or lawyer in Hartford, Connecticut. Nevertheless, his unprojected energies and nobilities and grandiosities are perpetually assuming shapes of self-pity, yearning for enveloping love, and woman-worship; and although Pierrot is entirely too aware to mistake them for cosmic pains or enchantments of the heart, his sentimentalities threaten shamelessly to overcome him, and add immeasurably to his embarrassment. Hence his ideal self, the cruelly murdered "I-the-Magnificent," incapable of revealing itself in all its princeliness, gains satisfaction in the shape of revenge. It takes the exaltations of the subject emotional self, and very archly turns them into parody. Of melancholy soliloquy and philosophical dudgeon it makes a silvery music signifying nothing. (Rosenfeld 156–57)

Rosenfeld's analysis—or psychoanalysis—of the Pierrot figure, caught in a dilemma of desire for emotion and scorn for emotion, his potential for greatness thwarted, who seeks revenge in the parody of great human emotions—love, worship, sorrow—and so renders them hollow, is surprisingly close to the objections of new humanist critics, whose primary criterion for art is an affirmation of human values and the moral imagination.

Aesthetic involvement in Stevens' style, however, draws Rosenfeld into a dilemma of his own toward the end of his essay: he attempts to span both humanism and aestheticism in his final evaluation of Stevens. Articulating the humanist call for verbal simplicity and sincere emotion, Rosenfeld states that an "impulse in us bids authors be more simple and direct, and give completely what they feel; above all to advance from behind the curtain of language" (Rosenfeld 160). Yet he immediately confesses that "*Harmonium* remains one of the jewel-boxes of contemporary verse. . . . Stevens is revealed an almost impeccable craftsman. . . . his idiom [is] new and delicious" (Rosenfeld 161). Rosenfeld colors that "curtain of language" with an impressionistic sensuality which belies his desire for the poet to "advance from behind it" for any reason, let alone simplicity and directness.

Rosenfeld's dilemma reflects a confusion of standards in the assessment of poetry which can roughly be termed the battle between emotion and craftsmanship. Other critics, too, faced this evaluative choice in dealing with Stevens' poetry. Some, like Edmund Wilson, could commend Stevens' brilliance of craft and sophistication of thought, yet complain about his lack of feeling, choosing over Stevens a poet like E. E. Cummings, who, though stylistically "an eternal adolescent," is "not chilled; he is not impervious to life" as Stevens is (Wilson 102–3). For Wilson, Stevens' ultimate irony lies in the surface richness of a poetry that conceals inner "aridity" of feeling; the portrait is not unlike Rosenfeld's Pierrot. Louis Untermeyer also denounced Stevens' poetry as frigid, claiming, "There is little of the human voice in these glittering lines," and taking a predictably firm stand in favor of those poets emphasizing "passion" rather than style (Untermeyer, "Five Poets" 160).

Mark Van Doren also raises the question of audience in regard to Stevens' ironic attitude. He sees Stevens as one of a handful of "wits" in twentieth-century poetry but questions the durability of a humor which is "tentative, perverse, and superfine. . . . it will never be popular. . . . Mr. Stevens will never be much read" (Van Doren 400). Despite the obvious failure of Van Doren's prediction, he does reveal an implicit criterion of popularity and communication which informed much criticism averse to Stevens' style. It was a theoretical stance directly opposed to Riding and Graves's theory of the "pure burlesque" of modernism and the general avant-garde drive toward a complexity irreverent toward public taste or intellect.

Edna Lou Walton's essay "Beyond the Wasteland" attempts to mediate between Stevens' complicated, apparently private irony and the needs of his readers. Walton sees Stevens as the last in a line of "Wasteland theory" poets, having to deal with the "emotional ennui" of the modern age which was described by Eliot and left for future poets to explore. For Walton, Stevens' "problem" in the light of this legacy is different from Yvor Winters' "hopelessness" or Archibald MacLeish's return "in desperation to the desert." By contrast, Stevens is a "poet of the senses," so "What was he to do in death valley?" (Walton 263) His poetic answer consisted in exploring every emotion, every mood with "full realization of its several anti-moods; . . . No feeling is more than acknowledged before it splays out into a dozen different and antithetical feelings" (Walton 263). Rather than limit himself to one emotion—or none—Stevens explores the difficult simultaneity of all emotions, the unresolved contradictions inherent in love, beauty, imagination. For Walton, Stevens' seemingly super-refined style is at once appropriate, necessary, and redemptive: "Stevens's highly mannered, technically superb verse is so written because it best expresses his particular creative imagination: to this mind no simple statement is possible, every word has innumerable associations. This poet is sincere in being insincere. . . . His sincerity lies in his attitude. Moreover if Stevens is over-refined, it is only because we still measure refinement by the normal bluntness preserving the ordinary man for his mechanical world—not by the truer instrument of the sensitive imagination. Refinement is all we have today of exuberance and vitality" (Walton 264).

Early critics receptive to Stevens could herald his use of irony as a regeneration of language, a revitalization of intellect, and the exhibition of a mature world view. But the polemical confrontation between tenets of "humanism" and "aestheticism" continued in Stevens criticism and in the working out of a viable modern poetics. The New Critics' treatment of Stevens needed to exercise a careful redefinition of morality in aesthetics, the nature of artistic communication, and the function of poetry in the modern age. But early advocates of Stevens had laid valuable groundwork for subsequent theory. Their delimitation of his uses of irony introduced an important pattern in a modernist attitude which needed to express and accommodate, confront and survive the new twentieth century.

*Piece the world together, boys, but not with
your hands.*
—Wallace Stevens

Not Doctrinal
in Form Though
in Design

In 1930 the confrontation between the humanists and antihumanists reached its apex in the publication of two successive collections of essays—*Humanism in America,* edited by Norman Foerster, and *The Critique of Humanism,* edited by C. Hartley Grattan—in which Stevens was cited as a central example to illustrate opposing views. The exchange drew into confrontation such names as Paul Elmer More, Irving Babbitt, and Stanley Chase as representatives of the new humanism, and Allen Tate, R. P. Blackmur, Kenneth Burke, Yvor Winters, and Edmund Wilson, who joined forces to oppose the excessively conservative brand of humanistic literary evaluation. It was a conflagration which had been gradually stoked for years, from the rise of the new humanists in life, letters, art, and education during the 1910s and the reaction to their policies from various groups who either opposed what they viewed as Puritanism and censorship or attempted to provide alternative solutions to the modern advance of scientism and materialism.

The new humanism, led by scholars Irving Babbitt, Paul Elmer More, and Stuart Pratt Sherman, originated from a deep concern with what these thinkers saw as the degeneration of the modern age from traditional spiritual and philosophical standards into relativism, materialism, determinism, and the respective danger and decadence of literary naturalism and romanticism. Humanists opposed relativism in all its forms—from William James's pragmatism and his breakdown of a subject-object dualism in philosophy to the romantic glorification of individual instinct and impulse. The latter, for the humanists, elevated primitive, "natural" man (the Bergsonian concept of élan vital) over the "higher self," the "inner check" of spirituality and discipline which Babbitt termed the *frein vital,* and so eliminated that element which distinguishes the human being, which makes humanness. Irving Babbitt in particular called for the development of the "ethical imagination" and its employment in art to raise humanity toward the ideal and the universal, rather than lower it into the "intoxicating cult of individualism" and an homage to the flux of experience. The "right use" of art for the new humanists was as a tool for the spiritual and moral elevation of man and for the underwriting of the universal norm.

At the farthest extreme from this classical and Johnsonian aesthetic were the romantics. In Babbitt's view, "with the elimination of the ethical element from the soul of art the result is an imagination that is free to wander wild with the emancipated emotions. The result is likely to be art in which a lively aesthetic percep-

58

tiveness is not subordinated to any whole" (Hoeveler 39). In the romantic redefinition of nature from the classical idea of order and balance to a sense of impulse, freedom, individuality, and feeling, Babbitt saw an essential ethical irresponsibility and a relativism dangerous to civilization and society. These "philosophers of the flux," as the new humanists called them, drew endless condemnation for their amoral "indulgence" in aestheticism. As an alternative criterion for art—and one which was to arouse the opposition of Tate, Burke, Winters, and company—the humanists posited "higher universals" as the true test of art. Their aesthetic was based on the classical notion of mimesis, the ideal of art as the "imaginative portrayal of the universal experience of a uniform human nature" (Hoeveler 52) in antithesis to the "lamp" of romanticism, which advocated individual imaginative and expressive freedom. Babbitt set his ideology in distinct opposition to the aesthetics of Kant's *Critique of Judgement,* which announced the autonomy of art and the "disinterested satisfaction" of the aesthetic experience, which separates art from the concerns of science, morality, or utility (Hoeveler 53).

If these tenets of humanist aesthetics and their articulation in Foerster's *Humanism and America* drew argument from such critics as Tate, Blackmur, Wilson, and Winters, still there were points on which the two sides agreed. Both were alarmed at the cultural state of modern America, at the advance of scientism in thought, materialism in life, and the danger of romantic excess in literature. Both advocated a discovery of stable standards for criticism and aesthetics. Yet these younger critics from the South addressed these issues instead with an aesthetic based on expressive form, the autotelic nature of the artwork, and the uniquely qualitative nature of the aesthetic experience.

In *The Critique of Humanism* the young New Critics attack the humanists on—and with—their own terms. Yvor Winters' essay "Poetry, Morality, and Criticism" establishes a new defense of poetry by using the humanists' own concern with the moral nature of art. Winters considered the criteria for good poetry to be intensity, complexity, and the "victory" of form over the difficulty of experience. Form, however, here suggests more than mere stylistic perfection. The poem exhibits a moral attitude toward experience, and the stylistic, formal control of a poem reflects the spiritual control of the artist. Winters uses a number of modern artists to make his point: "The spiritual control in a poem, then, is simply a manifestation of the spiritual control within the poet. . . . The laxity of the one ordinarily involves the laxity of the other; the rather limp versification of Mr. Eliot and of Mr. MacLeish is inseparable from the spiritual limpness that one feels behind the poems, as the fragmentary, ejaculatory, and over-excited quality of a great many of the poems of Mr. Hart Crane is inseparable from the intellectual confusion upon which these particular poems seem to rest" (Grattan 306–7). Poetic form stands as both self-control on the part of the poet and as an exercise of the will over chaos; "the moral discipline," for Winters, "is inherent in the literary discipline."

Winters stresses that the intellect goes only so far in

apprehending the value of the poem. The poem as an unparaphrasable intensity of experience demands a criticism which both fully exhausts the intellectual response and continues into the more emotive apprehension of art: "I am demanding . . . a 'subjective' evaluation of a body of experience. Unfortunately that is the only kind of evaluation of experience, literary or nonliterary, that is ultimately possible, and one has to have the training as well as the courage to make it" (Grattan 320). Winters criticizes both Paul Elmer More and Stanley Chase for their "bastard impressionism" toward literature, claiming that their approach skirts the intelligent view of art as art in favor of simplistic impositions of external, doctrinal concerns. He specifically attacks Chase's analysis of Wallace Stevens, heralding the poet as a representative of modernism, though Winters was later to express ambivalence toward, then censure of Stevens. About Stevens' "Anecdote of the Jar" Chase writes:

> Now the elements of this experience—the jar, its shape, color, and quality, the hill in Tennessee where it is placed, the behavior or appearance of the wilderness, the bird, the bush—stand doubtless in some kind of relation with each other in the poet's mind, have possibly certain symbolic values. Since we have no clews to these relationships and values, our mind is free to do anything it pleases with the bare gray jar, the hill, and the wilderness. This freedom, however, and any pleasure we may take in the separate images, in the rhythms, or the placing of the words, are not sufficient compensation for the state of uncertainty and slight irritation in which we are left. Very likely the little poem is meant to suggest

nothing more than the superiority, to an intensely civilized person, of the simplest bit of handicraft over any extent of unregulated "nature," but it has been seriously interpreted to me, by devotees of recent poetry, as, respectively, an *objet d'art,* a sex-symbol, and a burial urn containing the remains of a valued friend. And so it must remain, for me, not only like nothing else in Tennessee but like nothing else in the universe.

Winters responds with vehemence:

Any one at all familiar with the workings of Mr. Stevens' extremely ingenious and sensitive (and occasionally, be it said, profound) mind will suspect him of being too witty by at least a little to indulge in any such arbitrary symbolism, such "childish hieroglyphics," as Mr. Chase is bent on finding in his work. For myself . . . I have always believed that Mr. Stevens was writing in that poem about a jar on a hilltop. With that simple notion of the poem, I have succeeded in extracting from it a good deal of amusement and enjoyment, off and on, for some ten years. . . . There is no more reason for seeking a hieroglyphic significance in this poem than there is in *Lear;* Mr. Chase admits that Mr. Stevens has given him no clews to one, yet it does not occur to him that Mr. Stevens had in all likelihood no idea that the reader would go around looking for any. Mr. Chase has overlooked the poetry in an attempt to find the formula. (Grattan 326–27).

Winters concludes, for the whole New Humanist movement and its attempts at literary criticism, that although its ethics may be sound, "the arbitrary and mechanical application of these principles to organic experience, whether the experience be literary or non-literary, does not constitute a discipline but rather a pedantic habit. If one is to arrive at any valuable conclusions concerning literature one will have to begin with the study of literature, to discover its nature and master its means" (Grattan 331–32). He claims that the humanist position can and will be handled more intelligently by "such younger men as R. P. Blackmur, Francis Fergusson, Robert Penn Warren, T. S. Eliot, Allen Tate, and others, men who can incorporate these values into a richer experience" (Grattan 332–33).

Edmund Wilson, another critic who would later express growing doubts about Stevens' poetics, also looked in this collection to establish definitions of *discipline* and *morality* more relevant to literature. Wilson agrees with Winters that "fine workmanship itself must always convey an implicit moral" and that all genuine art demonstrates discipline, no matter what its implicit or explicit doctrine. Wilson taunts Paul Elmer More for narrowness of terminology regarding fin-de-siècle artists and the general nearsightedness and "intellectual arrogance" exhibited by new humanism:

> Yet the idea that, despite the cynicism of a Flaubert or the perversity of a Baudelaire, their novels and poems might show the application of an austere and triumphant discipline, the exercise, in dealing with the materials supplied them by their imaginations, of a rigorous will to refrain, and might thus fortify their readers as well as entertain them—this is something which Mr. More seems incapable of conceiving. He apparently believes that the only way in which it is possible for a writer

> to discipline himself in these bad days is to write literary criticism like his own and Babbitt's, which, though it is distinguished by thorough reading and sound writing, has obviously not required a discipline a fifth as exacting as that which has gone to produce some of the works of which it so superciliously complains. (Grattan 52)

But it was R. P. Blackmur who most carefully examined the concept of discipline in art. "The Discipline of Humanism" begins with a complaint much like Wilson's, that the humanists themselves have never achieved "discipline in terms of creative art, or in original work of any kind" (Grattan 237). Implicitly because of this deficiency of artists among their numbers, Blackmur distinguishes their form of narrow extrinsic criticism from criticism based on literary standards of the uniqueness, autonomy, and organic form of the art work. Blackmur believes that the humanists "censor such literature as does not fulfill, in the most obvious manner, the notion of a Humanist society. . . . human nature must be as they assert: any difference is wishful thinking, or the illusion of disillusionment; and further, every difference must be ruled out, so that what remains will be right and healthy, even if what remains is infinitesimal" (Grattan 244–45). The humanists' imposition of external doctrines onto art and their conception of a static tradition based on "antique principles . . . without embodying them in the civilization of today" leads, for Blackmur, to a dangerous removal from actuality. Blackmur calls instead for an aesthetic paradigm based on experience, one that is intelligible, useful, and relevant to life and art (Grattan 249–51).

The issue of a qualitative, experiential paradigm for art is one Allen Tate takes up in the collection's most rigorously reasoned article, "The Fallacy of Humanism." The central fallacy Tate exposes is the spatialization of time—a fallacy of which, ironically, the New Critics themselves would later be accused in postmodern analyses of their work. Here Tate demonstrates the fallacy of seeing time as a logical series, as a quantitative abstraction of space, to be found in the humanists' tendency toward "infinite regression" to an ambiguous "authority" in support of their principles. This appeal to a mystical yet authoritative past "takes all the *time* out of the past and all the concreteness out of the present" for Tate, and invites a false concept of timelessness, just as naturalistic science becomes "timeless" in its detemporalization of the past (Grattan 145–46).

The qualitative element, for Tate, lies in life, not in abstraction: "Experience alone is the road to Quality. . . . It is experience, immediate and traditional fused—Quality and Quantity—which is the means of validating values" (Grattan 162–63). Tate's reaction against what he saw as the quantitative, absolute spatialization of time, values, and humanity itself ("to quantify nature is ultimately to quantify ourselves" [Grattan 163]) creates the basis of the New Critical aesthetic, an aesthetic influenced by the Kantian generative idea and defined by the assumption "that the work of art is, from first to last, the celebration of man's qualitative experience" (Handy ix).

In Kant, early New Critics such as John Crowe Ransom, Cleanth Brooks, and Tate found an apparent resolution to the problem of aesthetic standards in the segregation of literary and artistic language and knowledge from the rational, discursive, and conceptual formulations of science. The valorization of literature as a special ontological entity and a unique, nonconceptual form of knowledge, however, both resolved a number of critical issues and raised new ones.

New Critical rhetoric emphasizes its adherence to what Alan Wilde calls the "disjunctive" ironic mode in its stress on the unification of the seemingly disparate, the move toward formal closure rather than resolution, the concept, according to Wilde, of "equal and opposed possibilities held in a state of total poise . . . an indestructible, unresolvable paradox" (Wilde 21). As a result, the New Critical criteria for art involve complexity, inclusivity, and synthesis. Complexity—especially in the criticism of Cleanth Brooks—demonstrates an initial "sense of the world's disorder," creating a tension among elements. The greater this tension, the more intense, more concordantly rich is the aesthetic closure. Inclusivity (and its parallel trope of paradox) similarly imparts a "depth" to the artwork, but it is an "apparent" tension, as Wilde points out. At the root of New Critical rhetoric is ever that search for union, harmony, "mastered experience" (Wilde 23).

The "mastery" of modernist poetry has been identified primarily as that striving for the "fully ironic" poem which will itself withstand irony and "hover" in an Olympian, aesthetic completeness above (and against) the chaos of experience. The concept of an organic whole itself precludes encroachment of truly disparate elements: despite its complexity and inclusivity, the formal economy by which each part modifies the whole and is in turn modified by it creates an untouchable autonomy from life rather than true engagement. For Wilde, this paradigm epitomizes "orderliness" rather than order and constitutes in its disinterested removal a primary flaw in New Critical theory (Wilde 26).

But beyond the formal closure Wilde identifies lay a foundation of implicit belief in a metaphysical and humanistic order and wholeness which was increasingly articulated in practical criticism. It was an emphasis on what Edmund Wilson called "coherence *and* significance," beauty *and* relevance, or in R. P. Blackmur's phrase, "form and value . . . sensibility and substance." With form and content decreed inseparable under the expressive paradigm of the subject which reveals its "essence" through form, the order and closure of the work of art necessarily suggested deeper orders in the world and in human nature. Since imposition of order was taboo, these orders must be "found," implicitly existent in the subject in patterns that would reveal themselves if one only looked hard enough. It was not, then, "Ideas of Order" but the "World's Body" which was to be fleshed, not "Theory" but "Reason in Madness" to be revealed.

The emphasis on unity—a unity going beyond Wilde's sense of formal unity, it being of logical necessity ontological—affected Stevens criticism during these years, especially as Stevens himself developed a more theoretical poetry and prose which examined issues of order and invention. For many critics it would have been easier had Stevens ended his career with *Harmonium,* and in fact, a number of critics proceeded as if he had, skirting later works and continuing to identify the poet by tired labels of dandy, hedonist, consummate stylist, lutanist on gorgeous verbal strings. But by the time of Stevens' death in 1955, the body of his work and its attendant problems and contradictions for criticism could not be ignored.

R. P. Blackmur might stand as a virtual paradigm of changing critical attitudes toward Stevens' evolving oeuvre. Blackmur's criticism of Stevens spanned some twenty-five years, beginning with the celebrated article of 1932, "Examples of Wallace Stevens." In this early article, Blackmur establishes himself as mediator between critical camps, declaring both "those who dislike the finicky" and those "who value the ornamental sounds of words but who see no purpose in deriving sound from sense" wrong in their assessments of Stevens and in their general critical assumptions. Instead, Blackmur redirects criticism to standards of organic form, declaring that Stevens' seemingly eccentric use of vocabulary is employed not to obscure but to *"reveal* the substance he had in mind" (Blackmur, "Examples" 68, italics mine). Blackmur emphasized the importance of context in determining semantic value in the poems and stressed the unparaphrasability of the work of art, the purpose of which was to yield an inarticulate "shock like that of recognition," to create something new and previously unknown "which is literally an access of knowledge" (Blackmur, "Examples" 69).

Not Doctrinal in Form

In his analysis of Stevens' poetry, Blackmur focuses on such issues as ambiguity, tension, unity, irony, tropes and images and on the question of obscurity in modernist poetry, thereby creating a virtual prototype of concerns for subsequent New Critical analyses. Using the poem as its own context, he praises Stevens' "density" of language in contrast to E. E. Cummings' "absence of known content" and notes the two different types of ambiguity that result. Stevens' type he finds "so dense with being, that it resists paraphrase and can be truly perceived only in the form of words in which it was given" (Blackmur, "Examples" 69–70). In addition, Stevens' inclusivity and tension of opposites (Blackmur highlights the antitheses of elegance/nonsense, dissolution/resolution, ornament/statement) makes not only for the stylistic balance indicative of "the mood of Euphues" but for a particularly gratifying sense of aesthetic resolution when those antitheses are brought into formal harmony. In "The Emperor of Ice Cream," Blackmur illustrates the fusion of images of life and death, claiming a transformative function for this aesthetically complete poem: "If the materials were contradictory, the very contradiction, made permanent, becomes a kind of unison" (Blackmur, "Examples" 76).

Blackmur continues his examination of this inclusivity through Stevens' use of an irony which "recoils on itself," presenting a solidity of being beneath the illusion of seeming. "The light tone increases the gravity of the substance. . . . an atmosphere of wit and elegance assures poignancy of meaning" (Blackmur, "Examples" 79). For this critic, Stevens' poems stand as paradigms of organic form, poems which "mean" their tone and whose "single lines cannot profitably be abstracted from the context. . . . literal analysis does nothing but hinder understanding" (Blackmur, "Examples" 79). Blackmur underscores his point by comparing the tropes and images of Stevens' poetry with those in Eliot and Pound. He opposes Stevens' inclusive "elaboration" of details to Eliot's "condensation" of beliefs into "drastic cries" or Pound's distillation of sensory perception into visual images. Blackmur sees in both Pound and Eliot lines and images which exist independently of each other. Pound poses a series of formally simple visual evocations, and Eliot merely "places a number of things side by side" to establish idiosyncratically violent contrasts and the dramatic molding of "wholes out of parts themselves autonomous." Stevens, on the other hand, forges images which depend on the "syntax" of the poem itself, which exist fully only in organic interrelation with all other parts of the poem. Blackmur uses "The Snow Man" to illustrate this interdependence of lines and as an example of what might be called Stevens' aesthetic teleology: the poet "ends where he began. . . . his beginning has become a chosen end" (Blackmur, "Examples" 89).

Finally, it is a skill with poetic obscurity which secures Stevens' position over Eliot and Pound in Blackmur's canon. While Pound's poetry relies on historical and classical "facts" for its understanding, Stevens uses no "outside knowledge": the reader cannot use extrinsic formulas to "split" Stevens' poetry. Instead, Blackmur claims, "you need only the dictionary and familiarity with the poem in question to clear up a good part of Mr. Stevens' obscurities" (Blackmur, "Examples" 90). Like

Pound's, Eliot's obscurities refer to material extrinsic to the poem. Eliot alludes to the history of ideas and beliefs, using "digested" facts and references which demand that "the reader must know what it is that has been digested before he can appreciate the result" (Blackmur, "Examples" 89). But Stevens' "pure" poetry, relying only on its own context for understanding, survives in a virtually autonomous aesthetic universe of its own.

Blackmur concludes his essay with a reference to the transformative, transcendent function of poetry, the creation of a permanence which establishes a "new sensibility," a new aesthetic stability amid the world's confusion. Blackmur's touchstones for poetic analysis are form and value: a recognition of the importance of formal analysis of the work at hand, yet the knowledge that formalism is "never enough" in apprehending that complete experience, that "hold-all . . . for the patterns of possibility" which is the poem. Throughout this collection he commends an "ironic" mode of thinking in criticism—and, implicitly, in poetry—rather than a "doctrinal" orientation, "ironic" thought being that which successfully "holds conflicting ideas in shifting balance, presenting them in contest and evolution, with victory only the last shift" (Blackmur, "Examples" 273).

Blackmur's conditions for the existence of art assume the term *composition* in his next essay on Stevens, "The Composition in Nine Poets: 1937." Of these nine, only Wallace Stevens and Conrad Aiken are said to "show evidence of even aiming at composition," of using "the maximum resource of poetic language . . . [to] act with

71

unity upon the responding sensibility" (Blackmur, "Composition" 199). For Blackmur, composition is the main principle of the aesthetic gesture, the creation of a "new whole" combining both value and form, "substance and shape" (Blackmur, "Composition" 223).

Blackmur isolates Stevens and Aiken for their ability to demonstrate the necessary purposiveness in the writing of their poetry, the attempt to order and "actualize the experience of the imagination" and to give shape to the abstract values and meanings of the human experience. Furthermore, Blackmur implies that these meanings and compositions are to be *found* in the world: "It is always the poetic imagination that restores the speculative and abstract imagination to the condition of the concrete and the actual; because it is the poetic imagination that alone sees and feels the speculative at work in the composition of men and women" (Blackmur, "Composition" 223). Stevens' ability to uncover the necessary order in the world is summarized for Blackmur in the title *Harmonium*, "a slightly flavored word for an instrument to make harmony; harmony is more than musical—there is, or is not, a harmony of the gospels, and there is a harmony in all things seen, or grown, together" (Blackmur, "Composition" 220).

The quotation titling Blackmur's next analysis of Stevens, the 1943 essay "An Abstraction Blooded," echoes the conclusion of his previous essay, though the two were published six years apart. Those six years, however, brought about a change in Blackmur's perception of Stevens' work. The article, a review of Stevens' *Parts of a World* and "Notes toward a Supreme Fiction," attempts to appropriate the poet's more theoretical "rhetorical" verse into the old canon, with minimal success. Blackmur works more comfortably in interpreting Stevens' theory to suit his own premises. For him the three "phases" of "Notes toward a Supreme Fiction" ("It Must Be Abstract," "It Must Change," and "It Must Give Pleasure") represent, respectively, the idea of being, the adjustment to experience, and the final, triumphant "access of being." The final "pleasure," then, is a metaphysical sense of discovery, a perception of the ultimate harmony of "change in identity, identity in change," a sense of that same poise, order, truth, and unity upon which Blackmur's poetic rests.

To Stevens' actual verse, though, Blackmur finds objections. He complains that Stevens' relations between the "triad" of "the abstract, the actual, and the imaginative," though theoretically acceptable, are not derived from within the material but exist as a merely "formal" imposition of order:

> If [Stevens'] notes are united, it is partly by the insight that saw the triad outside the poem, and partly by the sensibility—the clusters of perceptions, and the rotation of his rosary of minor symbols—into which he translates it. There is the great unity and the heroic vision in the offing, and they may indeed loom in the night of the poetry, but in the broad day of it there are only fragments, impressions, and merely associated individuations. Their maximum achieved unity is in their formal circumscription: that they are seen together in the same poem.

Whether a poet could in our time go much further

. . . cannot be argued; there are no examples; yet it seems more a failure of will than of ability. Certainly Stevens . . . has been contented or been able only to make all his definitions out of fragments of the actual, seeing the fragments as transformations of the abstract: each one as good, as meaningful, as another, but bound not to each other in career but only to the centre (the major idea) which includes them. (Blackmur, "Abstraction" 299)

Stevens, says Blackmur, shows a decline in the transforming, metaphysical ability of his earlier poems. Quoting Stevens' own poem against itself—"These are not things transformed"—he posits rather that the poet is "establishing a piety of the imagination with the effrontery of repetition" (Blackmur, "Abstraction" 300). And though the result of repetition, the creation of aesthetic intensity, at times suffices, Blackmur considers these two works lacking in the "power" of a truly transforming and ordering insight.

Nor is Blackmur better satisfied in his next review, "Poetry and Sensibility: Some Rules of Thumb" (1948), which analyzes Stevens' collection *Transport to Summer*. Blackmur admits in the essay's opening that "not at all the same elements enter into a judgment done in 1948 that entered into the judgment of 1930 or thereabouts," but he claims that Stevens' style has changed, considerably for the worse (Blackmur, "Poetry" 272). Again Blackmur attacks the repetition which his earlier essay had found formally effective but an insufficient substitute for truly transformative poetry. In this essay Stevens' previously aesthetically intense verse has become "a poetry of hocus-pocus," one "unusually high with the odor of 'poets' and 'poetry'" (Blackmur, "Poetry" 274). And where once Blackmur commended Stevens' ability to articulate the "experience of the imagination," he now sees too many poems which, being too self-preoccupied, "hide or obliterate what the poet ought to see" and whose language often fails to "survive its uses into another life—the life it taps" (Blackmur, "Poetry" 273–74).

These complaints find their final forum in the 1955 article "The Substance That Prevails," Blackmur's closing devaluation of Stevens as a poet of "apprehension" rather than "comprehension," a poet who exists not unpleasantly but finally insignificantly in a verbal universe, exhibiting a nominalistic attitude which delights in naming and forming, without engaging underlying beliefs. "Stevens is not . . . a man of intellect," writes Blackmur. "When he tries for intellect, for the *ordnance* of concepts, his work becomes merely discursive and his syntax disappears into an obfuscation of sensation—indeed into a disorder of sensation. The grasping hand, too grasping, lets everything drop into a tumulus of shards" (Blackmur, "Substance" 95). This essay nonetheless gives credit to Stevens' style, the "permanent order . . . upon the violence of talent in the soul," despite the work's implicitly "involved but uncommitted intimacy" (Blackmur, "Substance" 107). Finally, Blackmur identifies Stevens as a connoisseur of a particularly solipsistic type of chaos,

a Mediterranean man with very little of the rage for order which inhabits and inhibits so many of our northern ancestors. His sense of order is the sense of what he does with his chaos; order feeds on, does not repel, anarchy; his order is, finally, his catholic self. His barbarisms are his own, too, because his violence is his own. He knows with respect both to order and violence that they spring from deep within himself and also from greatly outside himself. With his order and his violence he is at home; he does not have to resort to them. *In nomine, numine.* (Blackmur, "Substance" 105)

Although Blackmur concedes Stevens' skill, this final essay, taken with the critic's evolving response to Stevens' work, demonstrates the difficulty of fitting Stevens into an aesthetic designed to disclose a metaphysical unity beneath the unity of disparate formal elements within a poem. Stevens' early poetry was easily received into formalist readings, for it so readily satisfied the aesthetic interest in semantic and imagistic complexities in both verbal and tonal play. But Stevens' later work, "devolving" as it were into theory, provided greater problems for both formalist critics and those critics of transformation, such as the later Blackmur, who, though respecting formal craftsmanship, still demonstrated a desire for unification and transcendence, for an aesthetic which could move beyond "coherence *and* significance" into a type of "significant coherence," beyond formalism to the suggestion of underlying order in human beings and the world.

There were some critics for whom the purely formal criteria with which Blackmur had begun did remain a valid focus for evaluation throughout, particularly for the evaluation of Stevens the "stylist." Some early supporters continued their somewhat impressionistic accolades for Stevens' technical virtuosity. Marianne Moore praised the "repercussive harmonics" of the poems in her *Predilections,* which collected three reviews (1937, 1943, 1952), each expressing an unchangeably favorable—if rather superficially analytical—impression of Stevens. William Carlos Williams, too, in his "Comment: Wallace Stevens," written on the occasion of Stevens' death in 1955, stresses mainly the stylish elegance of language and meter which "keeps us reading without the aid of any profundity of thought that may be there" (W. C. Williams 237). In fact, Williams specifically singles out the "joy" of Stevens' early verse, in which "words dancing across the page" established a unique excellence before "conscience overcame him" in the later, philosophical works (W. C. Williams 239).

This formalist disaffection with Stevens' later verse is not an uncommon reaction. Robert Lowell in "Imagination and Reality" similarly finds a falling off of cohesion. Lowell announces his attempt to combine Blackmur's appreciation of Stevens in early articles with the moralistic reticence of an Yvor Winters to arrive at "a calmer and more objective understanding of Stevens than is, perhaps, possible with any other contemporary American writer" (Lowell 400). For Lowell, that calm objectivity manifests itself in a structural, formal approach to Stevens, and it is with this evaluative tool that Lowell announces a negative move away from the early density of language and poetic organization, toward a simpler, looser style. "Notes toward a Supreme Fiction" draws Lowell's censure as "unsuccessful," structurally "sloppy," aesthetically "idiosyncratic," and "repetitious" (Lowell

401). Even when commending Stevens' skill, Lowell continues to write in terms of structure, poetic progression, and closure—usually complaining of Stevens' late "looseness" of style, though he does praise "Esthétique du Mal" for its inclusivity of theme and tone (Lowell 402).

Some formalist critics avoided the full scope of Stevens' verse altogether, in favor of analyzing one "representative" poem or simply illustrating a method. William Joseph Rooney is one such, who uses Stevens to demonstrate the merits of structuralist evaluations. In his 1955 essay "'Spelt from Sibyl's Leaves'—a Study in Contrasting Methods of Evaluation," Rooney proposes "to contrast a prevailing mode of criticism by explication with a mode of criticism more formally oriented." In opposing the structural to the semantic approach to poetry, Rooney illustrates his method with Hopkins' "Sibyl's Leaves" and Stevens' "Domination of Black"; the former, he says, fails under standards of structure, where the latter succeeds. While both poems exhibit the "identical general meaning"—the theme of fear of destruction— Stevens' work organically fuses "the constituent elements without either constraint or loss of identity." For Rooney, "Domination of Black," unlike Hopkins' poem, stands as an aesthetic totality, a "oneness" beyond a "rationalizable oneness." He writes: "The structure of 'Domination of Black' may not be reasonable, but it is credible. If it does not chart reality for the reader, it is itself real." Stevens works on the principle of "contiguity" rather than "causality," creating a structurally successful poem in which "something more has been said than actually is said." Rooney's essay is replete with forms of the word *perfect*. He seeks "perfection" of an aesthetic nature. He sees "joy in the speech as a perfect thing, whatever may be said of any experience with the realities pointed to by [the poet's] meanings." For this critical purist, "the difference between art and event is always absolute," and it is "the intense joy in a perfect object," the apprehension of the "autonomy" and formal precision of a poem such as "Domination of Black," which will redirect criticism into a more objective and fruitful course (Rooney 512, 514).

Not every formalist critic, however, was this exclusively textual. In many analyses of Stevens' work an introductory preoccupation with formal inclusivity and closure gradually led to intimations of further, deeper orders outside the poem's fictive word. William Smith, for instance, opens his 1955 essay "Modern Poetry: Texture and Text" with an assertion that "art has no absolute answers: its only answer lies in its being" (W. Smith 6). However, the essay quickly distinguishes the "text" (the poem's subject and substance) from its "texture" (how that subject is developed) and deplores modern poems in which texture is overemphasized; when "surface flash and dazzle becomes [*sic*] a thing in itself . . . where is the text?" (W. Smith 10–11).

Smith uses Stevens' work as an example of poetry in which texture and text work together. He examines the successfully organic poem "Arrival at the Waldorf," in which the complexity and antithesis of Stevens' chosen images are finally and harmoniously resolved: "There is no individual metaphor here which can be detached from the poem: every word exists because of every other; and all exist together because of the valid experience they communicate" (W. Smith 15). Smith insists on Stevens' success in the "transforming," "translucent," and "revealing" enterprise of poetry, an unveiling of "the true body of poetry which has always been human experience" (W. Smith 16).

The leap from formalism to structure as an analogue for deeper orders is tempting for Frank Doggett, too. Two of his many articles on Stevens—"Wallace Stevens' Later Poetry" and "Wallace Stevens and the World We Know"—demonstrate Doggett's formalism and his desire for the deeper affirmation of art. In "Wallace Stevens' Later Poetry" Doggett focuses on Stevens' "gift for the irrelevant," his ability to reconcile a number of disparate elements in final, formal closure. Doggett states at one point that the "mastery of the irrelevant by Stevens is especially a rhetorical achievement," suggesting formal rather than metaphysical closure (Doggett, "Later Poetry" 138). But in his general statements on the purpose of modern poetry precisely that element of human desire for closure enters: "By its engagement of irrelevance in the purposes of form, literature represents the concern of our age to impose by will an order on the appalling and countless litter of existence" (Doggett, "Later Poetry" 137). In "Wallace Stevens and the World We Know," Doggett's interpretation of deeper values becomes more explicit. After a long formalistic discussion of Stevens' technical development of imagistic and conceptual elements, Doggett comes to a final conclusion

that "the values in his poetry are those of warmth, summer, love, nobility, reality, light, life as opposed to cold,
denial, hate, fantasy, pomposity, sterility, blackness,
death" and that Stevens celebrates the instant, full
human life in an attitude of love toward the universe
(Doggett, "World" 371).

This straining toward a revelation of human values in
poetry beyond the purely formal values surfaces repeatedly in the idea of the formally complete poem as analogue of an intrinsic or essential coherence in its subject.
In this sense, the poem as synthetic whole suggests a
deeper world order, reflecting the reality of an orga-
nized universe. Some critics addressed this metaphysical
issue directly, especially in their evaluation of Stevens.
John Crowe Ransom's *The World's Body* articulates most
clearly a position which might be called metaphysical or
ontological irony. Ransom discredits "romantic" poetry,
"heart's-desire poetry . . . [which] denies the real world
by idealizing it" (Ransom, *World's Body* ix). Instead, poetry should project "the act of an adult mind" which
does not attempt to change or idealize the world, but
tries rather to "realize the world, to see it better" (Ransom, *World's Body* x). For Ransom, the "fulness of poetry
. . . is counterpart to the world's fulness," a verbal apprehension and fleshing of "the world's body" (Ransom,
World's Body x). He corroborates his point by comparing
the abstract (and incomplete) knowledge of the world
which science affords us to that more "real" and harmonious world which poetry discovers and reveals: "What
we cannot know constitutionally as scientists is the world

81

which is made of whole and indefeasible objects, and this is the world which poetry recovers for us" (Ransom, *World's Body* x–xi).

In a chapter of *The World's Body* dealing in part with Stevens, Ransom analyzes the modern "Poets without Laurels" who have ignored the public demand for social, moralistic poetry, in favor of the "pure" aesthetic experience. Ransom uses the often-cited "Sea Surface Full of Clouds" as an example of poetry without morality, juxtaposing it to Allen Tate's "Death of Little Boys" to demonstrate two types of "pure" modern poetry; Stevens' poem, says Ransom, shows "clarity" and "objectivity," and Tate's employs "obscurity" with its more "emotional" subject. "Personally," Ransom admits, "I prefer the rich obscure poetry to the thin pure poetry," but both strive for the poetic autonomy he seeks to illustrate (Ransom, *World's Body* 61).

Ransom's argument shifts from this celebration of what might be called poetic "specialization," however, and concludes with a call for poetry which demonstrates greater fusion of various elements. At one point, these elements include the union of "beauty with goodness and truth," whose "dissociation . . . is unnatural and painful" in poetry (Ransom, *World's Body* 72). A later chapter, "Poetry: A Note in Ontology," sets up the paradigm of "three types" of poetry: poetry of things, poetry of ideas, and "metaphysical" poetry, which fuses both types into a new and harmonious whole. Ransom calls this poetry a kind of "miraculism," representative of the *Dinglichkeit* of things, the transcendent essence, the concepts made actual (Ransom, *World's Body* 142).

In his later essay of 1955, "The Concrete Universal," Ransom employs Kant to explain the poetic bridging of the apparent dichotomy between determinate nature and the inner, free, moral and purposive world of man, singling out moments of finding or glimpsing a purposiveness in nature, a harmony between man and the world, an at-home-ness. Furthermore, the apparent dichotomy between the imagination and the understanding, the natural/free versus the moral/ordered, is reconciled by poetry which succeeds in the Coleridgean "balance or reconciliation of opposite or discordant qualities," thereby achieving beauty and import. The primary poetic vehicle for Ransom is metaphor, the "way to the homeless moral Universal," and he cites Stevens' poem "The Motive for Metaphor" as a consummate example of this theory (Ransom, "Universal" 400). Ransom's emphasis is consistently on the transformative nature of poetry—not as an imposed harmony, however, but rather as suggestion of a deeper world order and the discovery of underlying synthesis and purpose.

Although Ransom seems to have mentioned Stevens only perfunctorily, if complimentarily, other critics attributed to Stevens' verse precisely that "miraculism" of the "metaphysical" which Ransom had heralded as true poetry. Babette Deutsch calls Stevens "not the mystic but the metaphysician in love with this world," echoing Ransom's claim that for the truly "metaphysical" poet this world "is the best of all possible worlds." Deutsch, further, sees Stevens' poems as attempts to build a "transcendent analogue" to the world; she concludes by comparing the poet to God in analogous creation, with the implicit assumption that order and purpose reign in both "universes"—macro- and microcosm, poem and world (Deutsch 269). Joseph Duncan, too, affords Stevens a number of pages in *The Revival of Metaphysical Poetry*, pointing in particular to Stevens' "metaphysical" use of paradox, which creates the sense of poise, balance, order (Duncan 182–86).

Other critics, though not explicitly mentioning the metaphysical aspects of his poetry, also isolate Stevens' reflection of a world order in the poem. Louis Martz, in his essay of 1950, "The World of Wallace Stevens," establishes the dilemma of homeless modern human beings, alienated from a sense of the elemental, who must rediscover sustenance in and relationship to the world. The "war" between the mind and reality "must be resolved: this," says Martz, "is the poet's mission" (Martz 95). Resolution becomes a primary issue in this essay, and again it moves beyond formal or aesthetic resolution toward the actual apprehension of closure and order in the universe. Martz refers to Stevens' "Nomad Exquisite" as a demonstration that "the world is a unity . . . as the poem itself achieves unity and growth." And again, in Stevens' "The Red Fern," "we have a picture of a world in order" (Martz 97).

This analogue between poem and world, moreover, is seen to be a discovered one: "Amid this 'moving chaos that never ends,' order is thus found by the poet in moments of supreme awareness. . . . The affirmation is the momentary experience of unity and stability" (Martz 98). It is, in Martz's crescendo of evaluation, "the thing grasped in its radiant essence, the full, clear, white,

pure, dazzling realization of the world and all things in it
. . . the original Idea of the thing, or the thing as it
should be . . . essence." And further, "Such perceptions
are hardly to be planned, but they come to the man
who trains his imagination to perceive them" (Martz
99–100).

Throughout, Martz emphasizes the discovery of essence and pattern, of an underlying resolution to the
apparently "meaningless plungings of water and the
wind." Stevens, he believes, exhibits this "dedication to
the mission of the poet in the modern world" (i.e., the
discovery of resolution), but he has "limitations" in this
regard, which "place him on a rung below Eliot and
Yeats." Stevens offers "no all-embracing solution: his
search for the still point is not so profound nor so broad
as Eliot's; his 'paradise of meaning' has none of the religious and ethical implications that Eliot's rose-garden
holds" (Martz 109). Martz's critical assumptions are everywhere evident: poetry embodies the "metaphysical"
aim of unveiling an underlying synthesis in a world of
apparent chaos. Although Martz's opinion of Stevens
was to change, his ambivalence in this essay was to be
echoed by more and more critics.

Bernard Heringman is another critic ambivalent
about Stevens' contribution. In a review of *The Necessary
Angel,* Heringman disparages Stevens' lack of systematic,
logical development, yet uses the poetic, associative tone
of the book's prose to lead into a discussion of dialectical
play in Stevens' verse. He points to Stevens' "explicit ontology," which moves toward the "supreme fiction" of
synthesis, the "flash" of recognition—for Heringman, of

metaphysical transformation—the reconciliation of the duality of mind and reality. Heringman points out that for Stevens, poetry "is a way of life and a part of life" during these epiphanic moments (Heringman 523).

In "Wallace Stevens: Platonic Poetry," Alfred Alvarez finds many of Stevens' poems disappointing, and his explanation of their failure reveals similar underlying assumptions in Alvarez's view of poetry. For Alvarez, Stevens' poems lack "inevitability," are too arbitrary, evidence "a poet's imagery," use images "chosen because they are, if nothing else, clear; there is no sense of their having chosen themselves" (Alvarez 128). This implicit belief in a type of organic imagism radiating from the subject at hand makes for the tensely ambivalent tone of this essay. Alvarez concedes that at moments Stevens, too, "has great feeling . . . for the truth that lurks below the changing surface of appearances" and participates in "a moment at which [things] come truly alive: the moment at which they are caught in all their subtlety by the imagination. . . . And this is not a projection of the poet's self. It is a moment of purity when what is grasped is neither the commotion at the surface of the thing observed nor the commotion inside the observer" (Alvarez 130–31). Alvarez's wish for that essential "purity" and wholeness to be discovered under the "surface" confusion is further evident in his descriptions of Stevens' "best" poems as "lucid," a type of "transparent" vehicle to ontological truth. He criticizes the rest for their distracting, "encrusted," or contrived rhetoric, declaring that they "hardly exist below the level of style"—

again demonstrating an attitude which wants to see through to clarity and resolution.

Lloyd Frankenberg's *Pleasure Dome: On Reading Modern Poetry* attempts to extend this metaphysical sense of poetry's function into the realm of religion and faith. The sense of an order present in reality is evident throughout. "We perceive [beauty]," writes Frankenberg, "not by escaping the confusions and distractions of the present, but by observing them until their relationships fall into place" (Frankenberg 8–9). Poetry's purpose is "less to *represent* than it is to *enter*" its subject; modern poetry in particular should provide this sense of immediacy and simultaneity, the "experience of totality" which stands as "the resolution of apparent antithesis" (Frankenberg 12–13).

Frankenberg, unlike Alvarez, sees this resolution throughout Stevens' work. He progresses chronologically through Stevens' oeuvre, demonstrating the formal, organic closure of poems in *Harmonium,* seeing the idea of metaphor developing in "The Comedian as the Letter C" and reaching its culmination in the poetry of "living." The Stevens/Crispin figure finds "the constant and unpredictable interaction of reality and imagination . . . active and passive at once . . . a fiction paralleling life" (Frankenberg 215). Similarly, in "Sunday Morning" Frankenberg sees Stevens resolving "an uneasy antithesis between philosopher and poet," moving into later resolutions between appearance and reality in "The Man with the Blue Guitar" (Frankenberg 218). Here, being and seeming alternate to the point where the alternations achieve fusion in an equipoise, and "we give up the distinction entirely. . . . Poetry, Stevens seems to be saying, is the special case that brings together the other special cases and reveals their astonishing unity" (Frankenberg 225).

In a section of his book titled "Theories of Resemblance," Frankenberg approaches the issue of Stevens' "irony of ironies" in *Parts of a World* and *Transport to Summer,* where Stevens presumably reveals reality to be finally unseizable by the poem; however, Frankenberg interprets this rather as a leap toward belief than an admission of failure. The critic identifies this sense of reality with Zen—"an apprehension behind all apprehensions, a figment of figments; something sensed as unchangeable behind all change." At this point in Stevens' career, Frankenberg claims, the search is for "a stability that endures through all change and yet is created *by* change"—in short, the disjunctive paradox which results in synthesis (Frankenberg 236). And again, this closure must be found, not made: the "irrational moment" which is poetry may *seem* to transform from without but is in fact the world "truly perceived . . . by the whole man" (Frankenberg 264). Frankenberg concludes by attributing a religious impulse to this kind of poetry, claiming that "Stevens' poetry fulfills and exceeds Matthew Arnold's critical prophecy" that art would replace the religious impulse in its upholding of metaphysical closure and order (Frankenberg 267).

While a number of critics were examining the mimetic power of poetry to reflect metaphysical or world order through its own formal order, others saw in Stevens' po-

etry the reflection of a different significant "wholeness."
For these critics the exclusive subject of modern poetry
is the human experience—the mind itself rather than
the "world's body." William Van O'Connor, for example,
in his essay "Tension and Structure of Poetry," demonstrates how similar were the assumptions of the "metaphysical" and the "humanistic" critics, yet how different
their conclusions could be. O'Connor uses Stevens'
"Peter Quince at the Clavier" as an example of a modern
poem which fulfills criteria of inclusivity, tension, and
the use of antithesis for the purpose of a final resolution
into an "instantaneous whole" (O'Connor 563).

O'Connor, too, calls this process metaphysical, but he
describes it as a technical "multiplicity in unity," an expression of the human need for order: "The metaphysical mind of necessity seeks expression of its felt
complexities in the language of image" (O'Connor 567).
For O'Connor, finally, the poem's subject is the "experience," the "thought-situation," the human perception
and response rather than an apprehension of any external or transcendental "reality" (O'Connor 571).

Observations on the poem as a reflection of human
reality and experience also seem preoccupied with the
idea of resolution, wholeness, and completion. Just as
the new humanists emphasized the "whole man," the
"balanced" self, so too in a number of different forms
did these critics search for a synthesis in poetry of the
human experience. One such was Randall Jarrell, who
saw reflected in Stevens' poetry "the grandeur possible
to man" and the evidence of the whole man as the
"glory" of the universe (Jarrell 343). But here too Ste-

89

vens elicited differing views, and the advocates of his humanism found an outspoken antagonist in Yvor Winters.

Winters, named "The Logical Critic" in Ransom's *The New Criticism* and commended by Cleanth Brooks for being "logically rigorous . . . intelligent . . . a powerful corrective force," openly employed his own brand of moralistic criticism, which elicited denigration from other critics who deplored his dogmatism and his doctrinaire application of moral standards to art. Winters, coining and elaborating the concepts of primitivism and decadence in literature, identified certain elements and themes in the poetry of Wallace Stevens as hedonistic and attributed to them "the rapid and tragic decay of the poet's style." Winters saw the "cultivation of the emotions as an end in itself" in Stevens' early verse, and although he admired some individual poems (Winters declared "Sunday Morning" to be "probably the greatest American poem of the twentieth century and . . . certainly one of the greatest contemplative poems in English"), he believed this limited theme of hedonism had led to ennui and finally to the decay of Stevens' craft and career (Winters, "Stevens" 89–90).

Winters—likening Stevens to Poe in the pursuit of novelty, sensuality, the "sublime end"—points out the lack in Stevens' "doctrine" of "the possibility of the rational understanding of experience and of a moral judgement deriving therefrom"; Stevens' poetry, thus, stands in direct opposition to Winters' own neo-humanistic preoccupation with the rational/moral element in humanity (Winters, "Stevens" 93). Further,

Stevens' "hedonism" altogether precludes the application of a moral standard to art: unlike Winters' own belief that "the poem as an exercise in just feeling is an act of moral judgment," a poem like "A High-Toned Old Christian Woman" declares that "the 'moral law' is not necessary as a framework for art" (Winters, "Stevens" 97, 92). For Winters, in short, "to read any measure of neo-humanism into Stevens is as foolish as to endeavor, in the manner of certain young critics of a few years ago, to read into him a kind of incipient and trembling consciousness of the beauty of Marxism" (Winters, "Stevens" 95).

Winters sees a strain of decadent romanticism in Stevens, a composite impression assembled from his interpretation of the poems "Anecdote of the Jar" (which exhibits the romantic symbol of "the corrupting effect of the intellect on natural beauty") and "The Comedian as the Letter C" ("dealing with a poet who begins with romantic views of the function of his art and who, in reforming them, comes to abandon his art as superfluous") (Winters, "Stevens" 98). Winters points to the self-mockery, or "Romantic irony," of Stevens' tone, the "Whitmanian form of a romantic error," of pantheistic delight in landscape and locale, and the "wilful semiobscurity" of "The Man with the Blue Guitar," which merely restates, he says, the romantic severance between the rational understanding and the poetic imagination. Instead, Winters returns to Stevens' "best" early poetry—predominantly "Sunday Morning," in which he can perceive the technical perfection, clarity, "controlled unity," tension, antithesis, and use of traditional elements necessary for a "great" work of art (Winters, "Stevens" 99).

Fifteen years after the publication of "Wallace Stevens, or, The Hedonist's Progress," Winters appended a "Postscript" çontaining a commentary on *Transport to Summer, The Auroras of Autumn,* and Stevens' critical essays in *The Necessary Angel.* Moving away now from the theme of hedonism, Winters' criticism is no less harsh in its assessment of Stevens' poetic dissolution: "The fundamental idea in Stevens' work would seem to be a kind of nominalism, the idea of a universe composed of meaningless and discrete particulars. . . . The hedonism which I discussed in this [1943] essay appears to have been an attempt to mitigate the cold horror of the nominalism" (Winters, "Postscript" 34). Beyond this nihilistic, antihuman interpretation of Stevens, Winters also takes issue with the philosophizing of Stevens' poetry, in which "his style is perverse or clumsy or both" (Winters, "Postscript" 35).

This sharp criticism was not an isolated case; a number of critics agreed with Winters' view of Stevens as antihumanistic and, therefore, secondary. G. S. Fraser, in "The Aesthete and the Sensationalist," echoes Winters on many points. Labeling E. E. Cummings the "sensationalist" of language and Stevens the invariable "aesthete," Fraser believes that in the poetry of both "some element of human experience or range within it traditionally thought of as central, is left out. Mr. Cummings and Mr. Stevens do not fulfill Matthew Arnold's function for the poet of strengthening and uplifting the heart" (Fraser 267). Fraser emphasizes the "lack of the highest tension"—that of human passions, human grasp of and contact with the world: "The world, for Mr. Stevens, that the poet lives in is the world that he chooses to shape by the arbitrary emphases of a detached attention—an attention not itself shaped by the compulsions, for instance, of hunger or love" (Fraser 271).

This lack of the "human" element allows for Fraser's cool reception of Stevens: "In one's heart one does not quite think that he is a 'great' poet in the sense that, say, Yeats and Eliot are 'great' poets" (Fraser 271). Interestingly, Fraser blames society (which "gets the poets it deserves") for nurturing poets like Cummings and Stevens, who alternately explore or transcend but who never truly *reflect* a humanistic wholeness. "Only a more humane society than we have seen for a long time or are likely to see soon," Fraser concludes, "will prove a proper stamping ground for the fully humanist poet" (Fraser 272).

Wylie Sypher develops another of Winters' points, the "Romantic affiliations" exhibited in Stevens' poetry, particularly in contrast to what Sypher terms "the recent vogue of the metaphysical." In "Connoisseur in Chaos: Wallace Stevens," Sypher attacks Stevens' "imprecision of thought," his "counter-point of the intellectual against the affective," and his antimetaphysical dissociation of sensibility, which establishes an essential rift between the human being and the world, between the fiction and the object (Sypher 83). Sypher cannot identify Stevens as humanist in any sense, for he believes that Stevens lacks the "necessary absolute," that he evades totality and cohesion, that his "composition too autocratically determines the form of the experience instead of serving as a coherence within experience" (Sypher 87). Stevens' tone, moreover, is one of absurdity (and thus comedy) rather than the requisite "irony," and Sypher implies that only "irony" affords a seeing through to stability and coherence rather than a glimpse into chaos.

On the other side of the controversy about Stevens' humanistic or antihumanistic themes was F. O. Matthiessen, who, while recognizing Stevens' love for "the life of the senses," nonetheless saw in him an example of the total humanist: "All of Stevens' later work has been written against the realization that we live in a time of violent disorder. The most profound challenge in his poems is his confidence that even in such a time, even on the verge of a ruin, a man can recreate afresh his world out of the unfailing utilization of his inner resources. The value of the creative imagination, of 'supreme fictions' in their fullest abundance, lies in the extension, even to the point of grandeur, that they add to our common lives" (Matthiessen 73). Hayden Carruth, too, saw that "Stevens' delight in language is concomitant to his entire vision, his argument. . . . we shall see more and more clearly how *humane* is the desire which has given us, in these poems, a delight that is interpretative of our world" (Carruth 293). Carruth singles out the element of "mastery"—both of the poet's craft and of the fluctuating world—as an example of the human ability and wholeness which Stevens conveys.

Randall Jarrell's essays on Stevens also place him in a humanistic tradition, but they show ambivalence toward

Stevens' ventures into "philosophy." In his 1955 review of *Collected Poems*, Jarrell singles out "To an Old Philosopher in Rome," claiming that in this poem "we feel that Santayana is Stevens, and Stevens ourselves—and that, stopping upon this threshold we are participating in the grandeur possible to man" (Jarrell 343). Jarrell emphasizes this sense of communication and elevation, the poem's "plainness and human rightness" and Stevens' ability to look "steadily at the object" with a Goethean tranquillity, interested only in the "sense of the whole"; in Stevens he sees a poet who "looks, feels, meditates, in the freedom of removedness, of disinterested imagining, of thoughtful love!" (Jarrell 344, 346) And although Jarrell warns of the danger of too much philosophizing—a flaw he criticizes in the more "inhuman" and icily rhetorical poems of *Auroras of Autumn*—he concludes with a paean to Stevens' essential humanism: "Throughout half this century of the common man, this age in which each is like his sibling, Stevens has celebrated the hero, the capacious, magnanimous, excelling man; has believed, with obstinacy and good humor, in all the heights which draw us toward them, make us like them, simply by existing" (Jarrell 351).

What can we derive from this emphasis on human and moral values in modern poetry? This central problem involving the function of the critic is discussed in the 1957 collection *Literature and Belief,* edited by M. H. Abrams, which addressed "the persistent struggle in recent criticism to save the autonomy of a poem, yet to anchor it again to the world beyond itself and to reengage it with the moral consciousness of the reader" (Abrams 9). For Abrams, this struggle takes the form of critical assumptions, among them:

—the cognitive function, which claims that the poem yields valid, if nonlogical, knowledge (Allen Tate's concept of "knowledge of a whole object," the "truth" of inner coherence);

—the poem as analogous to the world (Ransom's sense of the poem as mimetic of the "world's body" as "denser and more refractory" than the scientist's simplified image);

—a critical emphasis on theme, inseparable from the poem per se but nonetheless existing as "an ownerless, unasserted, nonreferential, uncredited, and thoroughly insulated something which serves nevertheless to inform the meanings of a poem both with their unity and their moral 'seriousness,' 'maturity,' and 'relevance'";

—the sense of poetry as an experience which "engages the whole mind," including morals, beliefs, and experiences yet which is read for its own aesthetic sake (Abrams 9–11).

Although Abrams admits, quite rightly, that this final point "looks very much like an attempt to have art for art's sake and eat it too" (Abrams 12), he goes on to explain the ability of the poem to include morality by being an object "formally complete, hence beautiful, and intellectually and emotionally satisfying" (Abrams 18). "The poet must . . . win our imaginative consent to the aspects of human experience he presents, and to do so he cannot evade his responsibility to the beliefs and prepossessions of our common experience, common sense, and common moral consciousness" (Abrams 28). The poet must, finally, admit to the need for a "human center of reference" for the endurance and greatness of poetry; poetry, in short, must return to its neo-humanistic function of "uniform" communication and relevance.

In a similar way, Cleanth Brooks's contribution to the collection, "Implications of an Organic Theory of Poetry," emphasizes the homocentricity of poetry. Poetry is, he writes, "distinctly man-centered in that it represents experience seen in the perspective of human values" (Abrams 69). *Human* nature becomes "at once the Source and Test and End of Art," and for Brooks this standard insists on coherence as the element underlying both poetry and humanity. He posits that poetry's function is a knowledge-giving "revelation of life" and a "revelation of ourselves. . . . the primary criterion to which it must appeal its judgments is some norm of the human psyche" (Abrams 76).

Louis Martz's essay "Wallace Stevens: The World as Meditation" concludes the collection with a detailed and insistent canonization of Stevens as the ultimately humanistic modern poet. Martz opens with a justification of this placement, claiming that Stevens' poetry answers the question "What is the nature of poetry in a time of disbelief?" The answer Martz reads in Stevens focuses on human creativity, the will, reason, and the imagination. He claims that Stevens' later poetry exhibits a *growing* concentration on man, and he sees it as central that the African "subman" of *Owl's Clover* has evolved into the Guitar Player, bearing with him "a language moving now with a tough intent toward the discovery of a self," the true "province of poetry" (Abrams 152).

Martz centers on the topic of "meditative poetry," using Stevens' own phrase, "the poem of the mind in the act of finding / What will suffice." However, he takes a number of critical liberties in defining the "genre" of meditative poetry from "implications" gleaned in Stevens' poems. Martz's derivations include such rubrics as: the poet must "make contact with men in their normal existence"; he must use a persona, or "projected aspect of himself" to dramatize the act of searching, meditating, and finding—and this in order to evoke a sympathetic response from the audience; the poem must reach a moment of "emotional resolution—for a moment final," a sense of closure and wholeness and transcendence (Abrams 155–56).

Martz compares the "meditative" poetry of Stevens to that of Donne and to Jesuit devotional exercises, which move through traditional stages: establishment of a setting, intellectual analysis, emotional resolution, unity, and devotion (or the process from memory to understanding to will). He quotes François de Sales's definition of meditation as "an attentive thought repeated or voluntarily maintained in the mind, to arouse the will to holy and wholesome affections and resolutions" (Abrams 160). Martz concludes that "Stevensian meditation becomes: attentive thinking about concrete things with the aim of developing an affectionate understanding of how good it is to be alive" (Abrams 160). For Martz, Stevens celebrates "the wonder of human consciousness" in a truly affirmative humanistic fashion, involving exploration, acceptance, and resolution.

From Yvor Winters' identification of Wallace Stevens' "rapid and tragic decay" to Louis Martz's vision of Stevens' resplendent ascent into humanistic salvation, critics ran the gamut of opinion—all within the basic evaluative confines that consider poetry an expression of human wholeness. This confusion about Stevens' poetry echoes the ambivalence of those "metaphysical" critics seeking reflections of world order, who similarly saw Stevens as either consummate penetrator or hedonistic connoisseur of chaos. Stevens' later verse afforded the formalists problems as well: William Empson, partial to semantic ambiguity, pronounced Stevens' poetry mere "airless" philosophy (Empson 521), and Randall Jarrell's praise for Stevens also at times faulted the poet for neglecting organic, aesthetic form in favor of "inhuman" rhetoric and philosophizing. All these advocates of wholeness and closure—whether formal, metaphysical, or humanistic—found Stevens' poetry a restless bedfellow with their poetics of inclusivity and completion. It was in 1964 that Joseph Riddel closed his survey "The Contours of Stevens Criticism" by intimating the possibility that Stevens offered a new poetry and a new poetics—one of rupture rather than closure, of suspension rather than resolution.

4

Preferring Text to Gloss: From Decreation to Deconstruction in Stevens Criticism

I think it a capital error to confuse "decreation" with "deconstruction" and to make Stevens' use of the concept an occasion to "deconstruct" Stevens' poetry in particular and modernist poetry in general.
—Roy Harvey Pearce, "Toward Decreation: Stevens and the 'Theory of Poetry'"

Stevens is engaged in an "act" of decreation, one dimension of which is the turning of language . . . back upon itself. . . . It is precisely because Stevens is so insistent on decentering or interpreting the myth of the center, even as he moves toward the poet's necessity of totalization, that he is the ideal poet for exposing the blindness of a formalist criticism. He is postmodern.
—Joseph Riddel, "Interpreting Stevens: An Essay on Poetry and Thinking"

One of Joseph Riddel's main observations in "The Contours of Stevens Criticism" was of the growing critical acceptance of and focus on the later poems, those which had puzzled, alarmed, or drawn censure from earlier schools of criticism. On the one hand, it seems almost as if the "search" critics perceived in these later poems paralleled a new search in criticism. On the other hand, the postmodern appropriation of Stevens beginning at this time demanded a critical strategy which not only would wrest the author from the New Critical hold but would venture farther in addressing all of Stevens' works. New issues were raised which in themselves might serve to undermine the conventional modernist view of Stevens as well as provide that more comprehensive—and therefore more powerful—new framework.

There was a questioning of the nature and function of language beyond traditional formalistic and semantic analyses and toward a concept of the mediate, insuffi-

100

cient, self-undermining nature of language. Such critics as Roy Harvey Pearce raised the issue of Stevens' "annihilation of art," now to be seen not as superfluous or pejorative poetic violence but as necessary stripping of the inadequacies of language and of the evasive "will to compose" in the human mind. There seemed to be a search to come closer to an "ultimate reality" beneath or beyond the mediate functions of language and poetry. Yet the nature of this "ultimate reality" itself was questioned. Critics divided—often within their own works—between seeing that reality as a possibility to be rationally *known* and seeing it as an existential self-creation, or *being*. The paradoxes in Stevens between flux and abstraction, life and stasis, became epistemological foci, and elements of reduction and negation in the later poems were no longer subject to earlier charges of escapism or banality, receiving instead serious consideration as philosophical and stylistic reflections of the modern imagination.

Riddel's essay addresses in particular Roy Harvey Pearce's theory of decreation, calling it a "striking thesis" which "provides a rationale for Stevens' breakthrough to the poetics of the future":

> Picking up Stevens' phrase, "modern reality is a reality of decreation," Pearce applies it to the later Stevens' "act of the mind," claiming that his search for an "ultimate poem" (or ultimate reality) constituted an act of imaginatively breaking down the commonsense structures of reality by way of possessing a reality within reality, a pure abstraction. . . . In other words, those late difficult poems of Stevens, as Pearce sees them, are processes of

> decreating the structure of things perceived, subjecting
> experience to a process of imaginative abstraction which
> pushes towards a grasp of the "thing itself," an ultimate
> reality. (Riddel, "Contours" 134–35)

Riddel's essay grapples with the question of "being" versus "knowing," self-definition versus apprehension of an external *Ding-an-Sich* in Pearce's interpretation, revealing crucial assumptions about the nature of language underlying each critic's stand. Pearce early in his writings establishes the mediate nature of language as a limit to human knowledge, which *can,* however, be surmounted. He identifies the "decreation" of language and of language's distortions as the motive behind Stevens' "annihilation of art" in the late poems, his attempt to strip away the human "will to compose" in order to apprehend reality directly. Riddel, on the other hand, sees no exit from the "uncomfortable knowledge" of our mediated understanding. Instead, he focuses on the "truth" of the "evasion" of language itself, on Stevens' affirmation of limitations and qualifications rather than transcendence and totality: "Even though his last poetry evidences the wish to get beneath appearances to a thing-itself, even though its own style seems intent on pulverizing the metaphors and myths by which mind clothes reality, even though it occasionally asserts that the self must push itself toward the purity of the ultimate abstraction—even though all these are given voice, what remains vital in this poetry is the tension . . . between what is desired and what is finally accepted as possible" (Riddel, "Contours" 136). This split between desire and possibility, between totality and sufficiency in the human confrontation with language marks both the common foundation and the inevitable rift between two central critical paradigms for Stevens' later poetry—the decreative and the deconstructive—whose clash in the critical arena continues to reveal much about contemporary critical assumptions and their implicit criteria for Stevens' placement in the canon of American poetry.

Decreation is itself a volatile term, changing with its context, from its original use as a religious emptying of the self toward God in Simone Weil's work of Judeo-Christian mysticism *Gravity and Grace* through Stevens' use of the term to indicate modern secular reality in "The Relations between Poetry and Painting" to Pearce's distinctive appropriation of the term and the engagement of subsequent critics with the concept. J. Hillis Miller and Joseph Riddel are just two who adopted and adapted the term early in the development of their own analyses of Stevens and who demonstrate by the changing nature of their views how issues raised by the decreative paradigm implicitly anticipate a deconstructive reevaluation of modern poetics. To examine the issues this concept raised we can best view its evolving significance in the criticism of Pearce, tracing its efficacy as a theoretical "answer" to questions of language and knowledge explored in Stevens' texts.

Pearce's early articles set the groundwork, so to speak, for the adaptation of "decreation" as a solution to Stevens' often perplexing poetics. The critic's early focus is on Stevens' dilemma of imagination and reality as a dilemma of humanistic belief, a focus which continued to inform his criticism for three decades. In 1951 Pearce established his stance:

> Treating of the relation of the imagined to the real—figured recently as the war between the mind and sky—Stevens is treating of our problem of belief. Unlike an Eliot, he has refused to move out of our culture and into another and to seek a solution for the problem in the discovery of a "usable" form of belief. Rather, he has relied entirely on his own sensibility; he has tried to create the object of belief rather than discover it. . . . [Stevens] began by looking directly at the world which limits belief, continued by examining the possibility of ·belief and commitment in the face of that possibility, and has most recently been exploring the nature of possible belief . . . mature, considered belief in the reality which we have "as and where we are." (Pearce, "Wallace Stevens" 562)

For Pearce, Stevens' early poetry is an endless exploration of the dilemma that one cannot *know* anything "unsuffused by the light of humanity," which necessitates a reevaluation of the "real" in the context of human sensibility, the mind working on "the reality which it must inform" (Pearce, "Wallace Stevens" 566). Although in *Harmonium* and *Ideas of Order* "Stevens does not move from recognition of a problem to an attempt to work out a solution" (Pearce, "Wallace Stevens" 570), Pearce sees that "solution" finally reached in "Notes toward a Supreme Fiction."

Pearce interprets the three sections of "Notes" as a discovery of those "truths" which move the poet toward humanistic affirmation and a "resolution" of the paradox

104

of mind and reality. In "It Must Be Abstract," Pearce believes, it is humanity itself that exists as the Supreme Fiction, embodying and reconciling both the abstract and the particular. "It Must Change" identifies the changing nature of language as mimetic of the changing nature of reality and therefore as an authentic vehicle for its expression. In his recognition that the poet is "not hemmed in, but . . . released by reality" and change, Stevens appears both to celebrate life and to resolve the paradoxes of human limitation less fruitfully examined in his earlier work. "It Must Give Pleasure," finally, celebrates the human move toward belief, "inevitable" in light of this new "knowledge," fortified by a renewed acceptance and synthesis of "the rich pleasure of existence" (Pearce, "Wallace Stevens" 576).

Pearce's reading of Stevens affirms secular self-creation, the achieving of "form and wholeness," the reaching of an ultimate belief and an authentic apprehension of reality. His conclusions parallel certain New Critical preoccupations with the elevation of artistic formalism into metaphysical transcendence. "In the end," Pearce insists, "what issues from the poems is indeed a kind of estheticism, but as Stevens defiantly insists, the highest estheticism . . . locating, by means of the elegantly creative act, moral order in the world that men must make and suffer to make. . . . The reward . . . is knowledge and individuality—and a measure of freedom" (Pearce, "Wallace Stevens" 581–82). But although Pearce's transcendent terminology seems conclusive, his subsequent essays indicate the need to return again and again to

Stevens' difficult—and unresolved—concepts of authenticity, authority, self, and reality.

In his essay of 1952, "The Poet as Person," the paradox of imagination and reality is replaced by the dilemma of the individual and culture, the personality (imagination) struggling for precedence over a social order (reality) hostile to it but without which it has no existence (Pearce, "Person" 422–23). In "Stevens Posthumous" (1959), the problem is dressed in the metaphor of literary tradition, Stevens representing the "Adamic" poet in American letters, one of the "'Romantics,' bound and determined to push toward realisation that belief in the radical freedom of man which was one of the latent productions of their culture" (Pearce, "Posthumous" 67). For such, furthermore, "the balance between the claims of the other and the claims of the self could be only unpredictable" (Pearce, "Posthumous" 68). Throughout, Pearce continues to perceive a move in Stevens toward stability and certainty, "through the act of the poem to its essence; through poetics to ontology" (Pearce, "Posthumous" 69), believing that Stevens' ultimate certitude was that "somehow, somewhere, the transformative act that was the poem had itself to be transformed" (Pearce, "Posthumous" 71). Language, however, remained the problematic element in this transformative reconciliation between mind and world, imagination and reality. Even Pearce admits, "Poems, we must recall, are creations" (Pearce, "Posthumous" 81).

It is in Pearce's analysis of *Auroras of Autumn* that the concept of decreation surfaces as the most feasible paradigm with which to explain and resolve this dilemma.

Auroras of Autumn represents for Pearce the poet's "exercises in the exhaustion . . . of the urge to compose" (Pearce, "Posthumous" 75)—an urge which separates the mind and the world through the distortion of words. Pearce interprets Stevens' drive as the drive to abstract language out of existence, thereby enabling us to glimpse ourselves "truly" existing, without the separating function of language, achieving an "ultimate certitude that will derive from a confronting of the ultimate poem." For him, "the sum total of all poems—indeed, as Stevens was to declare . . . of all creative acts—is decreation and makes pass to the reality on which such creative acts are operative. Thus the poet as decreator apprehends reality as it has been before. . . . it could be overcome and transformed by the poet as creator. Decreation, then, is not so much a means to theorising about reality as to knowing it" (Pearce, "Posthumous" 76, 81).

Pearce's decreative move involves the stripping of language to reach and "know" reality, the undermining of traditional ideologies and culture in favor of "recreating" an authentic culture in terms of the fluctuating self, and success in achieving the oxymoron of "created belief" for modern man. Pearce places special emphasis on Stevens' last published poem, "A Child Asleep in Its Own Life," as a summary of Stevens' position. Stevens' character is "one who wills himself to be unnamed. He wills his own decreation, so that, beginning at the beginning, with the uncreated, he can come to know and teach what naming is" (Pearce, "Posthumous" 89). But in the end, Pearce believes that Stevens "perhaps de-

107

manded too much" of poetry in demanding "that poetry transvaluate itself by exhausting itself (which was its mode of being itself); that it become an instrument which, in all its decreative power, could blazon forth the pure power of creativity" (Pearce, "Posthumous" 89).

This intriguing, self-disassembling power of poetry, its decreative attempt to achieve the essential condition of its own being, anticipates much postmodern thought concerning the self-reflexivity of literary language. It is a concept vividly articulated in Roy Harvey Pearce and Sigurd Burckhardt's "Poetry, Language, and the Condition of Modern Man" (1960). Burckhardt begins the essay with a discourse on the modern poet faced with the "threat" of the disintegration of language, the sense that language is "a vast game of question-begging," and the correlative view of humanity as arbitrary, alienated, equipped with an inadequate medium for thought, expression, and being (Pearce and Burckhardt 2). Burckhardt traces a number of poetic responses to this "threat of disintegration," contrasting a Metaphysical poet such as Herrick—aware of, yet undisturbed by the fictionality of language—with a modern poet such as Hopkins, whose words call a far more disturbing attention to themselves as fictive entities straining to cohere.

If in a poem like "Spring and Fall/To a Young Child," Hopkins demonstrates "the linguistic impossiblity of that pristine innocence and sense of harmony in which all things stand side by side, inviolate, substantial and yet intimately related" (Pearce and Burckhardt 8), still Hopkins' dismay with language pales before Wallace Stevens' "merciless stripping." For Burckhardt, Stevens' "structured and mounting negation, until we have the thing 'itself,' untranscending, uncommunicative" (Pearce and Burckhardt 10), presents the ultimate modern dismantling of an inadequate language, a type of "linguistic existentialism" striving for both the irreducible nadir and the rebuilding of authentic meaning. In Stevens' "The Course of a Particular"

> we get the feeling that to say more than [the] barest of sentences is already too much, too risky, involving us, on the one hand, in fantasias of togetherness and on the other in a mode of speech so drained of all concreteness and felt reality that it seems to issue from a Hartford, Conn., office building. Anything that might smack of artifice, of vividness, is stringently avoided; even images are too much, it seems, because the human mind is so constituted that it takes images as metaphors and finds a specious consolation in the sense that things have, after all, a meaning, are related, cohere. It is this consolation Stevens deprives us of; he will not supply us with any props for our illusions. . . .
>
> . . . what we have here is a poem of radical doubt and analysis, in which the poet tries to get to the minimal, the quantum of meaningful language, out of which to rebuild the universe of discourse. (Pearce and Burckhardt 11)

Burckhardt insists that at least a "quantum" of meaning is still necessary, that some affirmation must evolve "which does not reduce the poet's whole enterprise to nonsense." This need for belief is reiterated in Pearce's response, which develops Burckhardt's sense of the paradoxical quest for an authoritative language, for that "pervasive Paradigm" which might serve as a new foundation for discourse. For Pearce, the answer lies in a "mutual mastery and submission" between poem and poet, language and modern man. Poetry's function is to reveal the human ability to free language from its conventional uses and so to imaginatively free itself by making language its own. Language, Pearce concludes, is "our prime instrument for being" in being our only vehicle for meaning, and he sees meaning and being as identical for man; language reveals both its own powers and ours in its ability to define and so create (Pearce and Burckhardt 30–31).

Pearce's affirmative views on language, self, poetry, and the decreative act are summarized in his 1980 essay "Toward Decreation: Stevens and the 'Theory of Poetry.'" In "Credences of Summer," Pearce finds an explicit indication of Stevens' ability to pass through negation to genuine meaning. He believes that the poem's fictive "singers" do in fact achieve the "hard prize / Fully made, fully apparent, fully found" by working *through* "that decreative mode that requires denial and doubt as a condition of achievement and certitude" (Pearce, "Decreation" 298). And although a poem like "The Well-Dressed Man with a Beard" ends with the claim "It can never be satisfied, the mind, never," Pearce insists that "in the great later meditative poems the mind— working through the decreative process—can indeed find its satisfactions" (Pearce, "Decreation" 298).

For other critics, however, this humanistic affirmation of imaginative power presented a facile sweeping under the carpet of issues of reduction and negation raised by the concept of decreation and an avoidance of its implications about modern language and poetry. As co-editor with Roy Harvey Pearce of the collection *The Act of the Mind* (1964), J. Hillis Miller had already taken a significantly bleaker view of the dilemma of modern man and the theme of Stevens' work, one which might have presaged his later turn to a deconstructive reading of Stevens. In "Wallace Stevens' 'Poetry of Being,'" Miller writes, "The evaporation of the gods, leaving a barren man in a barren land, is the basis of all Stevens' thought and poetry" (Miller, "Being" 144). Here, human beings are caught in a world informed by division and nothingness, a bleakness which permeates the relationship of the imagination to reality: "Imagination is the inner nothingness, while reality is the barren external world with which imagination carries on its endless intercourse" (Miller, "Being" 145).

A far cry from Pearce's perceived land of richness and celebration, Miller's modern world is characterized by homelessness ("The true reality has always been the wind and the indifferent glittering of an external world, a world in which man can never feel at home" [Miller, "Being" 144]), by the concealed nature of things ("Instead of being intimately possessed by man, things appear to close themselves within themselves" [Miller, "Being" 145]), and by the discovery of the nothingness underlying existence ("God is dead, therefore I am. But I am nothing. I am nothing because I have nothing, nothing but awareness of the barrenness within and without" [Miller, "Being" 145]). In this world whose only constant is the division between subject and object, mind

111

and world, reconciliation is impossible, and Miller sees Stevens' "search" as rather an endless attempt to escape from the conflict.

Focusing on the rupture between the imagination and reality, Miller commends Stevens' poetry as an authentic reflection of the irresolution of this situation: "Such poetry is not dialectical, if that means a series of stages which build on one another, each transcending the last and moving on to a higher stage, in some version of the Hegelian sequence of thesis, antithesis, synthesis. At the beginning Stevens is already as far as he ever goes. After the disappearance of the gods the poet finds himself in a place where opposites are simultaneously true" (Miller, "Being" 146). For Miller, Stevens' "chief contribution to poetry" is a mode of writing which can possess both extremes. Stevens' style exhibits an open-ended inclusivity—an aporia—of thought and image. It presents us with poems which violate organic unity in that they "begin in the middle of a thought, and their ending is arbitrary" (Miller, "Being" 147). Similarly, Stevens employs fragmentary titles, "emphasizing the broken, partial nature of the poem" and the lack of comforting connections between title and content. Stevens' poetry is, in short, a poetry "appropriate to the incomplete" (Miller, "Being" 147–48).

It is the very incompleteness of the poems which causes them to remain "true to life . . . a constant flowing of images which come as they come, and are not distorted by the logical mind in its eagerness for order" (Miller, "Being" 147). The longer poems, which "proceed in a series of momentary crystallizations or globulations of thought, followed by dissolution, and then re-conglomeration in another form" (Miller, "Being" 147), become analogies to Miller's own modified concept of decreation, a concept worth quoting fully to demonstrate its recognizable origin in, yet distinct move beyond, Pearce's use of the term.

> Within the "endlessly elaborating poem" . . . which is life, the same sequence of events is constantly happening over and over again. First something happens which "decreates," which destroys an earlier imagination of the world. Then man is left face to face with the bare rock of reality. . . . This clearing away is experienced not as a loss but as a gain. What is removed was a fictive covering of the rock, and what is exposed is the real in all its clarity. . . .
>
> . . . It is as if the poet were like the first man facing an "uncreated" world, with everything still to be imagined.
>
> This experience of coldness and earliness is only the start. The poet is not satisfied to confront a bare and unimagined world. He wants to possess it, and it can only be possessed by being imagined well. Man is inhabited by a "will to change" . . . which is just as unappeasable as his will to see the rock of reality exposed in all its bareness. The experience of decreation is followed by the reconstruction of a new imagination of the world. (Miller, "Being" 149–50)

But Miller goes on to describe the process of decreation/recreation as *endless*, lacking Pearce's final synthesis and satisfaction in "imagining well": "No sooner has the mind created a new fictive world than this 'recent imagining of reality' . . . becomes obsolete in its turn, and must be rejected. This rejection is the act of decreation, and returns man once more to unadorned reality. The cycle then begins again: imagining followed by decreation followed by imagining and so on for as long as life lasts. In this rhythmic alternation lies our only hope to possess reality" (Miller, "Being" 150).

Miller stresses this endless, unresolved motion of decreating and recreating as a possible accommodation of the Cartesian impasse, both in life and in poetry. In life, the ideal becomes the present moment, that instant "disencumbered" of the past and existing purely in its own being. In poetry, the goal becomes the grasping of the present. Stevens, Miller believes, captures this elusiveness of being and time in his use of "autonomous" images and phrases, each of which in some way "moves so rapidly it has beginning and ending at once. Instead of being fixed and unyielding, a solid piece of language interacting with other words, each image recapitulates within itself the coming into being of the moment and its disappearance" (Miller, "Being" 153). Stevens' "Poetry of Being" conditionally achieves cyclical decreation.

By 1980 Miller's views on Stevens had moved still farther from Pearce's decreative synthesis. In "Theoretical and Atheoretical in Stevens," he goes so far as to indict his earlier paradigm—and all paradigmatic criticism which presupposes one authoritative interpretation of poetry. Miller admits that "the vague outlines of Stevens' particular version of the ancient Occidental metaphysical system of concepts involving the presence of the present and the fleeting revelation of being in the vanishing of the instant" lures the critic—as it certainly

114

did Miller—to claim being as the fundament of Stevens' work (Miller, "Theoretical" 282–83). "Nevertheless," Miller now concedes, "the authentic voice of Stevens as a poet is not touched by such explanations. That voice is something unpredictable, savage, violent, without cause or explanation, irrational—as he always knew genuine poetry must be. . . . Continuously present, it is nevertheless a principle of discontinuity" (Miller, "Theoretical" 283).

The "new" root of Stevens' poetry, then, is no longer that fundamental expression of Being which Miller had outlined in his early essay. Instead, Miller now finds a disturbing and unnameable "enigma" at the heart of the poems. He avoids naming this mysterious "essence," claiming that if it is "seen through" theoretically, the poem itself fails: "To identify this disrupting element in Stevens' poetry, if it is neither imitation, nor 'Being,' nor merely the play of language, would require a full reading of his work. Even then, it may be that the identification would be a discovery of what cannot be named or identified in so many words, even figurative ones" (Miller, "Theoretical" 284). Miller ends his essay with the supposition that were we to try to "name" or ultimately explicate this "enigma," we would lose precisely "the essential poem at the center of things, which may be neither named, nor seen, nor possessed theoretically" (Miller, "Theoretical" 285).

Although a careful inconclusiveness and hermeneutic self-awareness marks this later essay, it is not yet fully deconstructive. Miller's interpretation of Stevens has only moved from the sense of an unfixed but nameable

115

concept of Being as the nucleus of the works, to the un-nameable but still implicitly possessed or "known" (else how could we "lose" it by theorizing?) "essence" of the poem, the "enigma." Miller's final critical turn is to see even this enigma as an utter unknown—one, further, which implicates the critic in a ruinous and self-under-mining game of linguistics. In "Dismembering and Dis-remembering in Nietzsche's 'On Truth and Lies in a Nonmoral Sense,'" Miller seems to have worked through the implications of his deconstructive turn more fully. Although this essay makes only a passing reference to Wallace Stevens, many of the concepts touched on in "Theoretical and Atheoretical"—the enigma, the abyss of interpretation, the inextricability of language from metaphysical concepts—are theoretically worked out through a reading of Freud and Nietzsche.

Miller begins with the enigma as the hypothetical site or "center" of the mind and of the text, which "cannot ever be clearly mapped," which can never be clearly spo-ken. Because of the nature of language itself, Miller writes, "'clear expression' must be qualified by saying that this clarity, for example in rational distinctions or in binary oppositions, is itself a trap for the unwary. . . . What seems at first so logical and rational [in the text] . . . breaks down into the illogical and irrational. It is a path to a blank wall the critic must in his own turn follow again if he goes far enough, not very far in fact" (Miller, "Dismembering" 43). The dissolution of the text's own meaning into its opposite, through the self-subversion of the figurative qualities of language, now makes the pre-sumed nucleus "a permanently unknown X . . . neither thought, nor thing, nor word" (Miller, "Dismembering"

44). Metaphor, and the metaphoric quality of language, rather than being a synthesis of thing and meaning, becomes instead an endless deferral, the more and more distant transposition of that "something outside human knowledge" which speech attempts to name. "The human word . . . is a labyrinth of figurative displacements around an unknown center" (Miller, "Dismembering" 45).

But even this labyrinth is no resting point, no safe (if provisional) structure protecting humanity from the unknown. Even in trying to discuss the situation, Miller points out, we become implicated in our need to work with language and therefore with a medium which is endlessly folding in upon itself, relentlessly subverting itself. Human "essence" takes on a bleaker definition, being "neither consciousness, nor 'spirit' nor 'selfhood,' but the power of making false transpositions" (Miller, "Dismembering" 47). All "truths," then, even those offered by critics attempting accurately to describe the situation of endless displacement, become illusory figures, constituting the final danger of modern dis-integration, beyond Burckhardt and Pearce's initial tentative description of the dilemma. Miller traces the condition behind the decreative impulse to find that the linguistic labyrinth truly "displaces itself everywhere. . . . Everything moves, wobbles, or stammers, as it does also in any commentary on the system" (Miller, "Dismembering" 50). The work of the critic now, as well as of the poet, becomes a "stammering," a "stuttering transposition of what may not be articulated clearly, namely the atopical unknown X" (Miller, "Dismembering" 51).

The implications of this view of language, involving

both literary and critical discourse, are radical for a truly revised view of Stevens' poetry and poetics. The working through of a theory like decreation—which points to paradoxes underlying the linguistic game, yet averts its far-reaching implications by continuing to rest on humanistic, metaphysical foundations—might be said to be one of the recognizable patterns of the deconstructive turn. Joseph Riddel, in a career of Stevens criticism spanning from 1958 to the present, undergoes many of the same reappraisals of the nature of language and the critical enterprise as did Miller, beginning with an engagement with the decreative paradigm and moving to its logical outcome in deconstruction.

Riddel, too, began with a series of interpretations of Stevens which revolved around the rhetoric of resolution, synthesis, origin, and presence. In his 1958 article titled "'Poets' Politics': Wallace Stevens' 'Owl's Clover,'" Riddel is preoccupied with an underlying stratum of "myth" in Stevens, an emphasis on "the universal human constant," which has the power to transcend the divisiveness of the modern situation. The essay analyzes Stevens' attempt to render poetry the antidote to political institutionalization. "Poets' politics" are, for Riddel, based on "ritual" rather than "doctrine," are essentially "not politics at all but precede politics and eventually allow men to live within political systems without capitulating to them" (Riddel, "Politics" 119). Riddel's explications here and in other early essays, however, are based on what Paul Bové would call an "unexamined" system of binary opposites which implicitly valorize one term—organicity/artifice, truth/falsehood, "genuine"/ imposed systems of order. Riddel emphasizes throughout the need for a "human constant," man's desire "to come into a harmonious relationship with his moving world" (Riddel, "Politics" 124).

Riddel interprets the poet's "rage for order" as a much-needed return to myth, that "changeless element," that archetype which is both stable and vital, abstract and connected to "the earth." Through myth (and implicitly through "genuine" art which draws on this fundament), reality and the human imagination can fuse into a true, transformative order incorporating both change and permanence. But in his analysis of Stevens' "Owl's Clover," Riddel finds his optimism thwarted in the poem's ambivalent ending. Presented with the choice of "portent" or "statue"—for Riddel, the choice of a metaphysical/spiritual or a secular/imaginative order—the poet rejects both. The rejection of the "statue" as a poetic symbol (which through the poem has come to represent art, imaginative energy, and humanistic affirmation) Riddel considers

> one of Stevens' rare moments of doubt in that greatest of human powers. . . .
> . . . If Stevens has begun with the idea of testing the possibilities of order presented him in the 1930s, he has ended by rejecting everything, including the imagination. Politically, this would be anarchy, and irresponsible. Poetically, it ends by denying poetry. Is this Stevens' accomplishment? Has complete skepticism of system and ideology led him back to the most primitive of exis-

tences? No, although the fact that such thoughts can arise is a possible indication of his failure. (Riddel, "Politics" 129–30)

Affirmation/doubt, order/anarchy, responsibility/irresponsibility, system/primitivism—enmeshed in a rhetoric which implicitly looks for and valorizes an underlying order, Riddel sees "failure" in Stevens' poetic rupture, in "what H. H. Watts calls the 'cul-de-sac' which 'often terminates Stevens' wonderful testimony to his chosen solution'" (Riddel, "Politics" 131). Elsewhere, though, Riddel finds Stevens more receptive to a humanistic reading. In a subsequent essay of 1961, "The Metaphysical Changes of Stevens' 'Esthétique du Mal,'" Riddel posits the Arnoldian claim for poetry as a surrogate religion, "capable of saving us." The poet effects this "salvation" by virtue of his language and the "ritualistic" use of what Riddel sees as the inherent ordering power of the word: "Language, of course, is clearly a form or order, and syntax a convenient arrangement of one's world. . . . The poet becomes the custodian of enduring values. . . . Poetry is a conservation of both language and values" (Riddel, "Metaphysical" 65). Riddel sees the modern world as a "tragic disruption in the moral continuum," and war as the central meaning-shattering event of the twentieth century, in which "things are dislocated from a natural order . . . [and] objects preempt man and disturb the continuum of humanistic values" (Riddel, "Metaphysical" 65). Throughout, Riddel appears to valorize what even Stevens' own "Of Modern Poetry" clearly abandons: in the "changed theater" of the modern world, Riddel still paces the empty stage of "natural order," the "continuum," and sacrificed "values."

Riddel's early concepts of stability, meaning, order, and preservation continue to inform his essays through the 1960s. Although he is careful to dissociate the function of art from metaphysical transcendence, nonetheless Riddel's aesthetically transcendent, "hovering" attitude is clear. Theories of art as a type of mystical paradox by which humanity can "resist and reconcile the vicious 'otherness' of reality" (Riddel, "Authorship" 129) reveal a groundwork of belief in the power of art to stabilize and remove. Riddel's interpretations through these years demonstrate assumptions about the ability of language to preserve values, reinstate the authenticity of ritual, and effect gestures of return: to nature, to origin, to the "innocence" of direct perception, the "purity" of vital myth and the emotional symbol. This rhetoric, while provisional, nonetheless repeatedly assigns to poetry its humanistic function as "collective" meaning, "human constant," and communicative "universal." The aesthetic experience represents a "psychic balance"; it is "a mysterious blend of subject and object" which exists to reconcile mind and world, comprising both permanence and flux, creating the "unity that satisfies desire."

"Immutable forms" are further discussed in "Stevens' 'Peter Quince at the Clavier': Immortality as Form," in which Riddel describes Peter Quince as the artist figure who "constructs out of the raw materials of experience the viable forms which will endure; he turns the beauties of flux into the immortality of art" (Riddel, "Peter" 308). In a similar vein, the poem's use of music successfully "symbolizes the attuned spirit, allows an aesthetic distance from which one can contemplate the precious object" (Riddel, "Peter" 308). The New Critical theme of art as icon continues in Riddel's "Wallace Stevens' 'Visibility of Thought,'" in which art is described as "reconciling human conflicts in the 'removes' of metaphor, which capture a reality lying somewhere in the perceptual tension between self and world" (Riddel, "Visibility" 483). Moreover, although man exists "always at the edge of reality, and any question he asks about it qualifies the answer he receives," Riddel believes that the meditative power of Stevens' poetry has even the ability to break us out of this "hermeneutic circle," since "the efficacy of meditation is its release of the self from preconception" (Riddel, "Visibility" 484–85). And elsewhere: "In the intuitive resolutions of meditation, the world loses its alien identity within the self—time . . . is removed from space and purified (made timeless in the self)" (Riddel, "Visibility" 487). Finally, "man and his world become one in the poem, the icon of order which is the single remaining form of spiritual order in a secular world" (Riddel, "Visibility" 491).

By 1972, however, Riddel's critical position had shifted markedly. In his review of Helen Vendler's *On Extended Wings: Wallace Stevens' Longer Poems*, Riddel uses a new theoretical framework based on Heidegger, Nietzsche, and Foucault to analyze Vendler's rhetoric of "presence." In so doing, Riddel reveals (to use Paul de Man's paradigm) much of his own previous "blindness" while achieving his "insight" into the mystified assumptions of critical discourse. Riddel opens his essay with a discussion of the "onto-theological tradition" in Western thought and language which has affected both criticism in general and Stevens criticism in particular: "Inarguably, the history of literature has been inseparable from the destiny of onto-theological language. And likewise the history of literary criticism. The language of Being or presence stands at the authoritative center of our thinking, and the varieties of dualism emanating from it compose the manifold of what was up to Nietzsche an unbroken western tradition" (Riddel, "Interpreting" 79–80).

Riddel examines the dilemma of modern poets and critics in their new context, deprived of a metaphysics of presence, yet still caught in the rhetoric of that tradition:

> Nietzsche's pronouncement on the death of God may well have ended the era of onto-theological metaphysics, as Heidegger says, but the rhetoric of that tradition lingers on. Our modern poets and modern critics still think in the language of primary being, and suffer from the alienation that Nietzsche's question poses.
>
> . . . What does it mean, then, when a modern poet like Wallace Stevens restores, or attempts to restore, man to his centrality? Has he ignored Nietzsche, and returned to Emerson, as some critics have claimed? Or has he become the Nietzschean poet, taking the language of presence and bringing it into question? (Riddel, "Interpreting" 80)

Riddel anticipates his own hypothesis: that Stevens is indeed a "postmodern," or Nietzschean, poet, *questioning* rather than affirming the tradition, attempting to undermine rather than to find "salvation" in the language of presence.

Vendler's division of Stevens' poetry into two poetries—the poetry of words and the poetry of the idea—signifies for Riddel the misdirected "initial Richardian split" which identifies the poem both as autonomous, autotelic "object" and as "a stage in the sequence of development," a step in a process of "teleological refinement." For Riddel, this New Critical attempt at a "rescue of 'value'" by "sanctifying" the autonomy of the poem informs Vendler's formalist standards of internal coherence and wholeness—standards, further, toward which she sees Stevens maturing through the course of his career, in a way that explicitly reveals an unexamined teleological paradigm (Riddel, "Interpreting" 81–83).

Riddel reveals his own new orientation, using the theories of Jacques Derrida to summarize his revised, deconstructive approach to Stevens:

Modern critical thought applies itself to received texts, bringing those texts into question, exposing the hidden assumptions of their language. This thought, says Derrida, derives from a recognition that the old texts or systems of thought are composed of a language of presence. The new thought brings that language into question, thus introducing the problematic of a "discourse on discourse." This critical language, however, must take the old terms, for it has none of its own. It proceeds by turning language upon itself. . . . Is it not possible that the difficulty we have had identifying the "themes" of our modern poets, or of rescuing them from their evident banality, is that we have confused their statements, have taken the concepts as concepts or assertions (semantics), and refused to recognize the radical nature of their self-qualifications (semiotics)? (Riddel, "Interpreting" 84–85)

Riddel redefines Pearce's *decreation,* that term which earlier had fascinated him as just that "rationale for Stevens' breakthrough to the poetics of the future." For Riddel decreation now points not to the discovery of stability and the authenticity of re-creation but to a fundamental and unavoidable absence at the "center" of language and the poem:

> Stevens is engaged in an "act" of decreation, one dimension of which is the turning of language, and in certain instances a familiar or even banal concept, back upon itself, by way of pursuing some origin at the heart of utterance—or to put it in the terms of one of his poems, to seek the unspoken word of the "central poem" that is at once proved and disproved (and thus displaced) by "lesser poems." In short, Stevens seems to sense a presence at the origin, a discoverable presence, but every penetration to that presence only reveals that the place is a fiction, an interpretation, and thus not an ultimate or supreme or central poem but only another lesser poem.
> . . . [The search for the center of reality] is a search, of course, that must repeatedly bring into question all other centers . . . and ultimately bring into question the idea of a center itself, until in the centerless center of the imaginative activity, of the poem speaking itself, we understand the significance of the poetry of "play." (Riddel, "Interpreting" 85–86)

As if to demonstrate the significant shift in his paradigm, Riddel returns to the example of Stevens' final "crystal" of "Notes toward a Supreme Fiction," an image which the critic had earlier used as a resonant symbol of synthesis and stability, the "apotheosis" (to use Riddel's term) of humanity by imagination (Riddel, "Notes" 40). Now, however, "the fiction of presence is revealed; the center of the crystal is a point of infinite refractions, a nothingness" (Riddel, "Interpreting" 91).

Riddel's paradigmatically postmodern Stevens is explored further in an essay of 1980, "Metaphoric Staging: Stevens' Beginning Again of the 'End of the Book.'" Here, a poem such as "Esthétique du Mal" begins to question not only the efficacy of language but the position of the writer, the possibility of the "self" as the new modern "center," concluding that "the self no longer governs language, but is governed by it" (Riddel, "Staging" 311). What results is "an emptying out of all those follies of a 'paradise of meaning' or transcendental signifieds that have accounted for the place of a self between sun and moon, as in a theater of proper images" (Riddel, "Staging" 311). Language is unveiled as an "assassin's movement," an undermining which murders the illusions of wholeness, a "dissemination" of meaning, and a negation of system.

Riddel examines the notion of the "book" as it engages Stevens, the paradoxical "notion that, as Derrida has shown us, bears within itself an *aporia:* the idea of the book prefigures or represents a unity that it at the same time produces and commands" (Riddel, "Staging" 316). For Riddel, "Notes toward a Supreme Fiction" constitutes "the great text of this writing against the 'book.' . . . it is a master text that masters nothing" (Riddel, "Staging" 316) but instead unfolds in an endless scrutiny of its own textuality. The inescapable figurality of language precludes any return to a "first idea," to that beginning which will be authentic and original ("immaculate"), or to the attainment of that ideal "metaphor that murders metaphor" (Riddel, "Staging" 318). But in order to begin at all, Riddel posits, one must "forget the metaphoricity of the sun [reality] . . . evoke the origin of poetry in a truth preceding language . . . producing the illusion of a moment when language and idea were one" (Riddel, "Staging" 319). This provisional forgetting in order to begin becomes that gesture which allows the writer to reinvent, at the moment he unveils, the fiction of origin.

This succession of paradoxical language traps continues throughout Stevens: the writer unravels previous mystified systems, only to substitute yet another unsatisfactory structure in place of his negation. Repetition, play, difference, and centerlessness constitute Riddel's image of Stevens: everywhere, the poet "empties out the dream of closure," deconstructs "the fiction of an absolute," and turns the "golden center" into the "violent abyss" which is the scene of writing (Riddel, "Staging" 325–26). "From 'The Snow Man' to the late discourses on discourse, Stevens projected a shudder through the 'whole shebang' of representation, the fiction of the book" (Riddel, "Staging" 327). Far now from the imaginative arena of humanistic affirmation and order, Stevens' work has become for Riddel that deconstructive "theater of trope," caught—and, says Riddel, *aware* of its own entrapment—in an endless play of figurality and deferral.

In the deconstructive paradigm of Stevens' works neither primacy nor synthesis nor paradoxical "poise" will suffice to explicate the poet's complex system of unresolved antitheses and open-ended play. But the deconstructive appropriation of Stevens demonstrates merely another turn in criticism, by no means a definitive or final resolution in the play of power and knowledge which informs the critical enterprise. Deconstructive paradigms like Miller's and Riddel's, though reviving previously marginal elements in Stevens' texts— elements of rupture, non-sense, flux—often succeed only in inverting stands while remaining fixed in the very framework of centrality in language and authority in criticism which they attempt to undermine. The recruitment of Stevens into a deconstructive perspective illuminates and emphasizes his concerns with language and the interpretive gesture in a way which implicates the critic as well; the space between literary text and commentary diminishes, becomes more dynamic, reciprocal, involved. As a gesture which take concepts introduced by earlier theories such as decreation and develops them to their radical ends, deconstruction's contribution to Stevens criticism may be just that significant transposition of literature to the "world" which Stevens sought—the mutual, if irresolvable, attempts of all linguistic enterprises to situate humanity within the perplexing play of reality, interpretation, and understanding.

5

Misprision and Disclosure, History and the Abyss: Rewriting Stevens into the Eighties

In spite of—or perhaps because of—the far-reaching implications of deconstructive criticism like Miller's and Riddel's, the practitioners of this recent turn in criticism have found it necessary to defend their version of Stevens throughout the seventies and eighties against new seizures of the poet by a variety of critical camps. The polemics over the appropriation of this poet have brought about in some cases a clarification of the deconstructive stance, in others an attempt to move beyond the enterprise of the "new rhetoric," and in still others a vigorous attempt to dismantle the deconstructive position—each camp using Stevens as both the weapon and the "hard prize, / Fully made, fully apparent, fully found," of its theoretical investigations. Moreover, the context of critical debate in the past two decades has widened into a self-conscious scrutiny of the process of canon formation and encompasses in many instances a redefinition of the concept of literary modernism itself.

129

A genealogy of contemporary debate might begin at what seems an unlikely spot, with the publication of Hugh Kenner's *The Pound Era* in 1971. Somewhat ironically, Kenner's remarkable dismissal of Stevens from the canon of modernist literature may well have occasioned Stevens' most strenuous reinstatement by way of countercriticism and response. Kenner's book, which fixed Ezra Pound monolithically at the helm of the modernist canon and dismissed Stevens' work as "an Edward Lear poetic pushed toward all limits" (quoted by Perloff 486), began to throw light on irreconcilable breaches among critics and their definitions of modern poetry. "[The] very real gap between Pound and Stevens—a gap that perhaps no inclusive definition of Modernism can quite close—had become apparent," wrote Marjorie Perloff in 1982. "The split goes deep, and its very existence raises . . . central questions about the meaning of Modernism—indeed about the meaning of poetry itself in current literary history and theory" (Perloff 485–86).

In her article "Pound/Stevens: Whose Era?" Perloff attempts to identify the assumptions behind two versions of the modernist poetic enterprise and to define the rift between them. The "Stevensians" and the "Poundians" of current criticism, she believes, have split over conflicting interpretations of modern poetry—as poetry of "thought" or as poetry of "technique"; the "what," she claims, is in contention with the "how" of the poet's discourse. The project of modern poetry as seen by Stevens' critical advocates (stridently enough, in fact, to constitute what Perloff terms an "anti-Pound myth") emphasizes the poet's task of addressing the difficulty of "belief and value in a world without established systems of truth" and creating instead the "sustaining fiction" of poetic truth. In contrast stands Pound's preoccupation with poetic style, his "attempt to master reality with *persistence of method* rather than with *persistence of thought*," the culmination of which technique in the *Cantos* remains, for Stevensian critic Lucy Beckett, "the saddest of modern defeats" (Perloff 487).

Perloff believes that the matter-versus-manner debate points to a deeper juncture in the assessment of modern poetry. She quotes a number of critics to demonstrate that the "desperately triumphant poetic humanism" of Stevens discussed by such critics as Harold Bloom, J. Hillis Miller, Helen Vendler, and Frank Kermode indicates an "Arnoldian . . . essentially Romantic view of poetry" (Perloff 489, 491) which valorizes the lyric voice and the "organic unity" of Stevens' verse and which implicitly seeks out a romantic "'mythologizing of self' that replaces history" and an "inwardness" leading to the apprehension of personal poetic truth (Perloff 502). In contrast, the Poundians privilege the rupture of lyric into the "serial," collagelike mixture of modes of the *Cantos* and the abandonment of poetic "inwardness" for a renewed attention to the "surface" of poetry: the move from thoughts and truths to structure and technique, with the words and things "speaking for themselves." In his supporters' view, Pound breaks out of the bankrupt heritage of romantic solipsism and into a consciousness of history and tradition in the search for external reality, the "assertion that we have not invented meaning" (Perloff 503).

In the end, the division becomes for Perloff the venerable split between romanticism and classicism, the Stevensians believing that the "best twentieth-century poetry . . . carries on the great tradition of Romantic visionary humanism . . . with a slight influx of French Symbolisme to add piquancy" (Perloff 504) and the Poundians regarding "modernism less as a continuation of Romanticism than as a very real rupture with it. . . . Surely it is no coincidence that Pound scholars have so often been classicists. . . . For all these critics, the Pound Era is the era when the norms of the Romantic crisis poem as of the Symbolist lyric were exploded" (Perloff 505). For Perloff, furthermore, it is Harold Bloom who commandeers the vanguard of the "Age of Stevens" critics in reappropriating Stevens as romantic—as she states in her parodic formula for Bloom's poetics: "(1) It must be Romantic. (2) It must question Romantic premises. (3) It must be Visionary Humanist" (Perloff 490).

Though Perloff's summary of Bloom's drift may be correct, the technique of his "rewriting" of Stevens in *Wallace Stevens: The Poems of Our Climate* (1977) was a far more complex and far more significant critical act than the easy placement of Wallace Stevens at the helm of an American romantic heritage. Bloom does instate Stevens as the culmination of Western poetic tradition, in sharp reply to Kenner, claiming that modern poetry inhabits an age "we might begin to call the Age of Stevens (or shall we say the Stevens Era?)" (Bloom 152). At the same time, however, Bloom wrests the method (strong reading) and the prize (Stevens) from other comers to the critical scene, most notably the deconstructive critics. In

an intricate method of rhetorical analysis, Bloom sub-
sumes the deconstructive tenet of "rhetoric as knowledge" in an elaborately inclusive theory of "rhetoric as
persuasion" and an examination of the transformative
process of signification. Bloom believes he is avoiding
deconstruction's rhetorical cul-de-sac while he is attempting, in a sense, to hoist that theory by its own pe-
tard.

In brief, much of the book draws on critical concepts
raised in Blooms's earlier works and combines them in
an exhaustive study of Stevens as American poet fulfill-
ing the romantic tradition of Emerson and Whitman.
Bloom's Emerson is a strong figure of pragmatic idealism, the new romantic, aware of the bankruptcy of the
sublime, yet substituting for it a new, willfully self-cre-
ated ideal. He sees Emerson's three-part poetics of fate/
freedom/power paralleled in the critical formula of
ethos/logos/pathos, a trinity pointing to the process of
articulation, the wresting of meaning from linguistic
limitations through the "strength of misprision." Emerson, moreover, prefigures deconstructive critics in his
awareness of the illusory nature of previously comforting symbols of unity and transcendence. "No discourse
ever has been so overtly aware of its own status as rhet-
oricity" (Bloom 12), claims Bloom, tracing in his first
chapter repeated instances of Emerson's ambivalence toward "comforting illusions" and his essential reductiveness. But Bloom stresses the ideal of a final ascent to
poetic "Power," a radically willed reinstitution of significance, an imaginative redemption derived from the
poet's own struggle into the act of expression.

133

Emerson, thus, is reductive and yet supplies the structure for a poetic rebuilding, a father figure for his creative descendants both to emulate and to rebel against. And Stevens supplies the figure of the consummate rebellious son of the Emersonian dialectic, a poet who successfully uses the weapons of trope to "willfully transfigure the Emersonian reduction." Bloom articulates the new system as follows: "In Stevens, we will see Emersonian Fate turning into . . . the First Idea. Transcendental Freedom in Stevens becomes the refusal to bear so dehumanizing a reduction. Power or Will in Stevens' mature poetry is the reimagining of a First Idea" (Bloom 27). Or in other terms, "Fate in Stevens is the First Idea, Freedom is the realization that the First Idea cannot suffice, and Power or Will is a finding of what may suffice, a revision of the First Idea" (Bloom 54). Through the Bloomian Stevens, the First Idea—in a revised, successful form—is recaptured through the poet's will to expression. Stevens becomes a figure of the redemptive strength of imagination and will to overcome a debilitating realization of entrapment and abyss and to find a successful resignification of the poetic act.

Christopher Norris writes that "Bloom clearly sees himself as doing for present-day criticism what Stevens achieved for American poetry" (Norris 120), or what is more likely, Bloom sees Stevens "doing" poetically what Bloom himself is trying to "do" in (and to) the critical arena. And what Bloom "does" for criticism—in terms of his "redemptive" gesture of the reversing will—is to redeem through radical will the deconstructive reduction of rhetoric to the untranscendable negative mo-

ment of aporia—to move, in short, "beyond deconstruction."

For Bloom the idea of rhetoric-as-persuasion must be
revived to parallel (and eventually overshadow) the deconstructive hobbyhorse of rhetoric-as-knowledge, for
the latter inevitably ends in a figuration of doubt,
failure, and absence, focusing only on the self-contradic-
tory, self-subverting nature of language itself. Against
this deconstructive "reduction," Bloom sets his criticism
to move beyond the "limitations" of such critics as Paul
de Man, allowing rhetoric (both critical and poetic) once
more to "transcend" the labyrinth of trope and reenter
the space of persuasion and individual will: "The issue
of the limits of deconstruction will be resolved only if we
attain a vision of rhetoric more comprehensive than the
deconstructors allow, that is, if we can learn to see rhetoric as transcending the epistemology of tropes and as
re-entering the space of the will-to-persuasion" (Bloom
387–88). For Bloom it becomes a question of opposing
to the limiting synchronic "asceticism" of deconstruction
a diachronic view of language as a transformational process, which includes considerations of tradition, association, intertextuality, and the "ancient identity between
rhetoric and psychology that is still being partly ob-
scured by that endless clearing or curing of the ground
now being called 'deconstruction'" (Bloom 396–97).
Through this and his final, elaborate theory of poetic
"crossings"—moments of psychic crisis or "negative moments" which the poet overcomes through rhetorical
shifts—Bloom's critical eye is continually on the writer's
ability to recuperate rhetorical power and significance,

to overcome (while recognizing) the deadening limits of language and the past.

Far from spearheading a Stevensian consensus, as Perloff suggests, however, Bloom's work evoked a number of reviews most notable for their extreme ambivalence. Scholars seemed eager to rescue Stevens from the imposition of this rigorously wrought critical apparatus, which promised to find Stevens' poetry "more truly and more strange" than ever before. Denis Donoghue commended Bloom's illumination of some aspects of Stevens, while condemning the inhibition of others (Donoghue 39). More strenuously, Ronald Sukenick tackled this "quirky" publication by calling it, on the one hand, "probably the best book on Stevens, though this isn't high praise," and, on the other, lamenting the "frequently apt theory and frequently inept Stevens explication" of this critical "provocateur" (Sukenick 634, 636). Perhaps the best illustration of how grudging was the acknowledgment of Bloom's work comes from Frank Kermode, whose rhetoric demonstrates the extremes of ambivalence the work elicited: "Bloom's interpretations and judgments of Stevens, extricated from their sometimes obnoxious packaging, nearly always strike me as right, and as having their own exactness" (Kermode 9). Yet the book's "unnecessary length, its libertine discursiveness and allusiveness, are partly a way of emphasizing the commentator's presence and his benign interpretive violence" (Kermode 9, 44). Bloom persists in "cobbling together overlapping 'systems' from philosophical, rhetorical, psychoanalytical and Kabbalistic odds and ends. . . . It is usually possible to translate even the toughest passages; but that does not make them less hideous" (Kermode 44). Finally, Kermode must face the dilemma of evaluation: "And now the time has come to answer the question, Who is Stevens's best commentator? And the answer seems to be, 'Harold Bloom, alas!'" (Kermode 44).

Among the varied responses, however, Joseph Riddel's "Bloom—A Commentary—Stevens" is perhaps the most perceptive on Bloom's attempt to outrhetoricize the rhetoricians in his oddly intra/contra-deconstructive endeavor. Riddel uses Bloom's book as a vehicle with which to examine the nature of the critical enterprise itself, commending Bloom's perspicuity in theoretical self-awareness but finally calling on the deconstructive strategy itself to undermine Bloom's evasion. Riddel begins by citing Walter Benjamin and Michel Foucault on the difference between commentary and criticism, undermining the traditional, mystified notion of "commentary" as a screen behind which much contemporary criticism continues to conceal its interested, provisional nature. Traditionally seen as a concern for the "primacy" of the literary text compared to the secondary "transparency" of criticism, commentary is "unmasked" by Foucault: "What Foucault calls the 'infinite rippling of commentary'—its desire to say what has already 'silently been articulated deep down' in the primary text, yet to say this 'never said' for the 'first time'—implicates commentary in a 'masked repetition.' Even 'simple recitation' translates, transcribes" (Riddel, "Bloom" 111). For Riddel, Anglo-American literature in general "tends to repress the contradiction and the 'play' and to present the relation of critical text to creative text in the guise of a simple, orderly representation, a humble criticism that effaces itself, becomes transparent, in the very moment of finalizing a commentary that is itself finalized and ordered by the priority of the creative text. American criticism wants to make the 'infinite rippling' of commentary into a fixed repetition, to mask its own 'masked repetition,' to proclaim itself 'valid,' a 'proper' 'description,' a description with (rather than without) place" (Riddel, "Bloom" 111).

This preface provides Riddel with a polemical foundation for approaching Bloom's work, which Riddel commends for standing in a far less disguised relationship to the creative text of Stevens than previous criticism had. Rather than offer a transparent revelation of "the" Wallace Stevens, Bloom's system has instead irritated conventional Stevensians in its clearly nontransparent, nonsecondary nature. Traditional commentators, Riddel points out, are appalled at Bloom's "audacity in placing the grid of his system upon the Stevens canon," making an intertextual play of critical and creative texts which "has touched (and contaminated) the rituals of commentary. . . . [Bloom] has claimed to see Stevens, if not steadily and whole, then centrally and totally—but at the center of a rhetorical prism that appropriates Stevens, *the* Stevens, overwriting him in a commentary that refuses to efface itself, that refuses the practiced humility of commentary" (Riddel, "Bloom" 111). Riddel identifies the ire of the Stevensians as a reaction to the obviousness of Bloom's critical appropriation: "It is Bloom's Stevens, and not criticism's fictionally *true* Stevens, *the* Stevens of some hypothetically neutral, transparent commentary. . . . So much for the masks of unmediated commentary; not to say, unmediated poetics" (Riddel, "Bloom" 112).

What Bloom calls into question, it seems to Riddel, is the issue of the original, privileged author altogether and the traditional enterprise of criticism to penetrate that "central" and "original" self behind the text. And Bloom's notions of misprision and intertextuality shatter the autonomy of the poetic text as well: "Bloom reminds us that texts are, after all, repetitions on which one writes 'masked repetitions' which have 'rippling effects,' and moreover, that the primary text on which the critic writes is itself a layered repetition, a weave of interpretations, a reading of *earlier* texts. This irrefutable Nietzschean complication has put the very notion of author/self in jeopardy, and routed the classical notion of hermeneutics" (Riddel, "Bloom" 112).

Compared to the "ventriloquism" of traditional commentary, which attempts to efface itself as the "voice" of the text, contemporary criticism, more aware of its own enterprise, "overwrites, displaces, appropriates the text," and Bloom does this no less than the deconstructionists he attempts to refute. "Bloom's system revises the poetic text as surely as any deconstruction. Bloom, then, begins from the foreign assumption that poetry is a discourse" (Riddel, "Bloom" 113). Nonetheless, he veers from the rigor of deconstructive evaluation of poetic language in that "he would try to provide a sanctuary, a privileged place for it" (Riddel, "Bloom" 113). Riddel, having found Bloom's "negative moment," proceeds to examine

his attempts at "restoration," at moving beyond an aporia of powerlessness into a reclamation of language and
will. In Bloom's attempt to appropriate (or "save") the
text from the deconstructors, he is in fact attempting to
restore the poetic self, placing the "troper" before the
"trope"—even though that "self" is now entangled in
"lines of succession, a struggle of generations . . . a
complicated history marked by the drama of conflict
and anxiety played out as a psychic economy" (Riddel,
"Bloom" 112).

Riddel surveys Bloom's complicated system of maps,
substitutions, poetic repetitions and crossings, tracing
his attempt to locate "the dialectical turn that allows each
poet to be 'orginal' . . . that accounts for the movement
within a poet's individual poems, within his entire canon
. . . and within the tradition of ancestors that his work
rereads" (Riddel, "Bloom" 114–15). Bloom's basic error,
Riddel finds, is his ultimate desire for authority, both in
poetry and in his own criticism:

> Bloom's celebration of the will to power of rhetoric, of
> the triumph of strong poets over their strong fathers, or
> the three-fold movement of the strong poet and strong
> poem in fragmenting the old vessels and putting them
> back together in a new arrangement, and his own insis-
> tence that his theory can eventually transume de Man's
> locating of the irreducible contradiction of language,
> chance all the risks of repeating what has had to be aban-
> doned by traditional criticism. For Bloom wants nothing
> more than to recuperate, perhaps for a final time, the
> primordial power that western poetry and criticism cele-
> brates [*sic*] in the form of loss. He wants to valorize a

140

language that has been denuded by modern criticism. . . .

 He seeks to rewrite the fable, to recompose a rhetoric that is real. . . . He cannot remain, or allow his poets' [*sic*] to remain, within the brokenness which must be produced with every effort to begin again, to be original. . . . So Bloom rewrites the critical fable, and does it within the fabulous coherence of an *ad hoc* dialectic, a daemonic invention. Bloom's system is so over*wrought* that it must reveal its own artifice: it is like a *dedale* with its false and self-consuming center. (Riddel, "Bloom" 115–17)

The strenuous conclusiveness of Bloom's "fable" becomes, for Riddel, both a revealing indicator of the desire for coherence underlying traditional modes of commentary and, as such, an invitation for its own deconstruction. Riddel indicates a number of points at which Bloom's system must be broken: his framework of postromantic epistemology (that "secularization of the theological vision of Transcendentalism" [Riddel, "Bloom" 118]), his unexamined valorization of speech over writing, and his desire to subsume all other systems into his own powerful and authoritative mechanism. Riddel suggests an authentic mode of intellectually countering Bloom's system through "rereading," while he commends Bloom's break from the paradigm of traditional "transparent" commentary. Bloom's critical system, he recognizes,

 cannot be simply denied. Nor logically unlocked. Like Emerson's rhetoric, as Bloom himself argues, it cannot even be deconstructed. But it can be reread. That is, Ste-

vens can be reread. Which will include a rereading of
Bloom's reading. Not in the way of the old critical argument, by a point-by-point refutation and a corrective.
But by a reading. I wonder how many critics will take the
trouble, or even concede its importance? And how many
will simply go on denouncing Bloom's enterprise, on the
ground that criticism must finally uncover *the* Stevens.
(Riddel, "Bloom" 119)

Whereas Riddel's strategy is to see Bloom as a kindred
spirit to the deconstructionists in the "unmasking" of
commentary, yet one who fell back into the desire for
authority which, Riddel implies, more rigorous theore-
ticians have had to abandon, Paul Bové confronted
Bloom—and his reading of Stevens—with significantly
less leniency. In the preface to *Destructive Poetics* (1980),
Bové questions the entire idea of tradition in literature
seen as a continuous, privileged interrelation among
texts; instead, he promotes a version of intertextuality
which insists upon "the open form of the destructive
language event which is the poem" and which sees all
"genuine" uses of language as existing in a destructive
mode "oriented towards the future in a discontinuous,
nonimitative relation to the verbal events of the past"
(Bové xiii). Bové uses this more radically disjunctive view
of the relationship among texts to analyze the failure of
a number of critics—specifically Harold Bloom, Walter
Jackson Bate, and Paul de Man—to confront issues of
poetic interrelations and the implicit problems of influence, poetic autotelism, and history.

Bate and Bloom (who makes use of Bate in tracing the
history of associationist psychology important to the the-

142

ory of *The Poems of Our Climate* [Bloom 397]), Bové says, both use unexamined genetic models to answer questions about literature's relationship to the past. Bate's trope takes the form of a linear development in the poet's historical neurosis from "a beginning of the burden of the past, its growth into a middle of paralysis, and its end or death in an awareness that the entire problem is a neurotic illusion" (Bové 5). Similarly, Bloom's theories derive from "the genetic metaphor and its variants—the myth of the Fall, the idea of origins, the language of loss and nostalgia, and the ultimate death of poetry" (Bové 7–8). Even Paul de Man neglects to examine his own formulas and presuppositions in crucial ways, failing, for Bové, in his unconditional belief in the authenticity of poetic language, in literature's constant awareness of its own fictionality. Bové quotes de Man: "Poetic language names this void with ever-renewed understanding. . . . This persistent naming is what we call literature" (Bové 44). But such a statement puts literature in a privileged position, sees it as eternally self-aware and constantly calling attention to the aporia beneath all language.

For Bové, instead, language itself is continual interpretation, and a new literary "history" must "include not only the series of critical misreadings of a given text, but also the interrelationships among poems as they are interpretations, deconstructions, of each other" (Bové 48). The "stripping of stability" from criticism *and* from literature is the necessary step away from all stability of privilege and continuity into the "radical flux" of discourse which does not discriminate among modes. Using Heidegger's "Phenomenological Destruction" to effect that step toward a more "authentic mode of interpretation," Bové emphasizes the hermeneutic awareness of the interrelationship between method and truth, between interpreter and text. "Truth," or uncoveredness, must be seen as continually falling back into hiddenness, true "speaking" into "idle talk," and the process of interpretation becomes an ongoing process of recovery and reclamation. The "disclosure" is, furthermore, not only of the thing itself but of our "relation to and involvement with the thing," which operates from the forestructure of our understanding. Authentic interpretation cannot escape this forestructure: in Heidegger's famous phrase, "What is decisive is not to get out of the circle, but to come into it in the right way." An awareness of the nature of our own interpretive enterprise and its limits, along with a conception of the interpretive/destructive nature of the text we are examining, informs Bové's poetic of "destruction."

With this groundwork of theory in place, Bové engages Stevens' work in a chapter titled "Fiction, Risk, and Deconstruction: The Poetry of Wallace Stevens." Bové sees the idea of "fiction" as the dominant element in Stevens' poetry: "Not only is the self and the other defined as fiction" in Stevens "but 'empirical reality' is seen to be finally devoid of transcendent certitude; in the last measure, we are left with nothing but 'fiction': 'The final belief is to believe in a fiction, which you know to be a fiction, there being nothing else'" (Bové 181). Yet for Stevens' critics, Bové explains, this concept of the fictionality of reality is seen not as radically as Bové would

144

expect but merely in the outdated light of "the Romantic and dualistic metaphysical tradition," which posits either a symbolist transformation of reality into internal order or the realists' concept of an empirical "reality" having primacy over the mind (Bové 182).

Bové takes on three major Stevensians—Pearce, Riddel, and Bloom—and examines them as emblems of particular critical fallacies in their approaches to Stevens. For Bové, Pearce reflects the "typical" attitudinal undercurrent in modernist criticism for which the "Romantic desire both for synthesis by dialectic and for the developmental metaphor underlie the perspective which causes these critics to look for a 'final' position in Stevens" (Bové 183). Bové summarizes Pearce's stand:

> Although Pearce defines himself in opposition to the New Critics, his language of continuity keeps him in essentially the same tradition. Pearce begins from the assumption that Stevens continues in the tradition of Romantic and American dualism and proceeds to argue that he brings it to culmination by achieving a kind of Kantian synthesis which posits reality in a "third term": the conjunction of self and outside world in an active perception of empirical reality. . . .
>
> The developmental metaphor of nineteenth century organicism and positivism dominates Pearce's discussion of Stevens. He sees Stevens' career as a movement from a clear beginning to a definite end which achieves synthesis and thereby eliminates the tensions which the unresolved conflict arouses. (Bové 182–83)

These residual images of synthesis and teleological completeness which Pearce illustrates haunt criticism as "variations of the myth of presence," variations which Bové also commends Riddel for unveiling in the latter's critique of Helen Vendler's *On Extended Wings*. For Bové, "Vendler's view of Stevens' poems as circles gathering 'beginning into end' and apotheosizing themselves as Absolute Images of verbal purity is the result of a circular argument which stems from the sedimented, reified, covered-over habits of reading Modern texts from a New Critical point of view" (Bové 184). Bové reiterates the necessity of hermeneutic modes of interpretation and understanding and claims that "Vendler, like the New Critics, is mistaken in attempting to avoid the circle. . . . Ironic criticism, which in its desire for infinitude and godlike hovering tries to deny what Kierkegaard calls 'actuality' and Heidegger 'existence,' naturally cannot help but be blind to the interpretive, i.e., destructive, aspects of poetic discourse and structure" (Bové 184–85).

Bové agrees with Riddel that Stevens is, in fact, engaged in the destructive enterprise of turning traditional discourse back upon itself. It is a view of Stevens as "archetypal 'ironist'" who "uses poetry to scrutinize its own origins until he finds that at the 'center' of poetry and all reality there is no 'presence'" (Bové 185). But Riddel too comes under Bové's censure by using the metaphor of search and discovery to define Stevens' poetic task. Although Riddel's belief that the "search" in Stevens reveals the centerlessness of poetry, by using the critical rhetoric of teleological finding or achieving, Riddel himself is inconsistent. Had he carried to completion the insight that this poetry scrutinizes itself by looking for its origins, he would recognize that the very metaphor of search, which he employs to describe Stevens' works, is also being turned back upon itself. It is by virtue of the awareness that there is no center that Stevens is able to rethink specific centered myths and metaphors and show them to be fiction in a radical sense in the early poetry. . . .

. . . Stevens does not learn by a failed quest for a center that center and therefore quest are meaningless. Rather, he actively employs the *telos*-oriented quest metaphor against itself not merely to show that there is no center but to test in fiction various poetic and personal myths and metaphors in a world with no firm point of reference. Herein lies the radical risk of Stevens' poetry. (Bové 186–87)

Stevens' poetic act is one of radical destruction of the "hardened" "truths"—acquired beliefs, myths, interpretations—which had inauthentically "acclimated man in the world . . . which had anthropomorphized and reified disclosure" (Bové 187). In this way, Stevens' poetry also "preempts" a critic like Harold Bloom, who attempts to ground poetic free play on a stable continuum and imply a final, willed transcendence into significance. Bové's Stevens instead "begins with a more complex sense of the issues at stake in reducing poetry to the free play of substitutions resting on a sure ground—Stevens, unlike Bloom, seriously questions his own 'first idea'— and . . . Stevens' poetry is often a destruction of the sublime as Bloom describes it" (Bové 188).

147

The poet, Bové believes, answers the problem of language instead through a Kierkegaardian employment of "mastered irony": "Stevens is free of the coercive genealogical myth of progress and the aesthetic myth of ironic hovering. Consequently, his 'tests' of various tropes and metaphors against the absence of center to reveal what is still positive and redeemable within the sedimented tradition are, as Kierkegaard says of Goethe, ways of 'making his existence as a poet congrue with his actuality. . . . The truth is that the particular poetic production is simply a moment'" (Bové 189). By revealing the fictionality of the static center, Stevens reinstigates discourse as a temporal act, as an occurring-in-the-world.

Bové sees "The Snow Man" as an example of Stevens' ability to trace the movement from the "comforting delusion" of anthropomorphization to the revelation of the nothingness at the "center" of existence:

> In the state *prior* to the reduction traced in this poem, "the listener" could only respond to the nothingness which exists by making it meaningful, by adding to it a sense of depth which makes it less "other." He refuses to let the "other" stand as it really is, as a mystery he cannot understand. He demonstrates no "Negative Capability," but, instead, transforms the "other" into something possessing "human" qualities, that is, readily interpretable along the lines of habitual, anthropocentric patterns of expectation which reflect the "listener's" own image back upon his senses.
>
> . . . After reduction, the listener "beholds" more clearly that his pathetic identification with a seemingly

concrete other is a fiction at the root of which lies "nothing." As well, he learns of a more profound relation between himself and the other. He is "nothing himself," that is, he is ontologically identical with the other insofar as they are both part of "what-is" existing in and by virtue of "nothing." . . . He senses the falsity of the dualistic separation of *res cogitans* and *res extensa* and sees the primordiality of Being-in-the-World, alongside the World, as a structure of his own Being. (Bové 190–91)

This reading of the poem sees it piercing fictions of self, presence, center, "the soothing concepts of the transforming sympathetic imagination and of the unique self" (Bové 191). The poem even deconstructs itself to reveal itself as a fiction based on nothing; it "refuses analogy, metaphor, and correspondence. . . . the poem is not even an allegory of the failure to name the center. . . . Stevens is willing to decenter even the most assuring myths of self, of the ability of poetry to reach some final position which will give it a unique value, and of the comforting aesthetic possibility of reading a poem simply as a narrative allegory of its own failed, fictional nature" (Bové 192–93). Discontinuous, engaged in the "risk" of the ultimate deconstruction of itself as fiction, Stevens' poetry demonstrates a reinterpreting of the tradition both to destroy its obscuring myths and to allow what has been "covered up" (to use the terminology of existential phenomenology) to emerge. "The poems refuse all sense of finality or simple reversal. Instead, they remain open to whatever may appear as the poem itself subverts habitual structures and expectations" (Bové 194).

The avoidance of the "still-point" of resolution or finality is most evident for Bové in "The Comedian as the Letter C," which he considers a fully "deconstructive" poem set in sharp contrast to traditionally teleological quest poems such as Wordsworth's *Prelude*. The conventional quest-structures move toward the "*telos* known from the beginning," the "visionary goal, an end which will be a *final* truth or idea toward which they can read and write comfortably, secure in the knowledge that they have found or will find the still-point outside the game" (Bové 195). They are "designed to move both the quester and the reader of the text away from the disintegrated, vacuous uncanniness (*Unheimlichkeit*, 'not-at-home-ness') of this fallen world of metaphorical difference, *back* to a mythic state of unity which is concealed by 'consciousness'" (Bové 197). But in counterpoint to this quest-desire for a return "home," a recuperation of prelapsarian unity, Stevens' "Comedian" reveals precisely what the invariable failure of the quest motif reveals: "that you cannot go home again, because there is no home to go to" (Bové 198).

Crispin is just such a romantic quester for teleological return—one who never arrives at his "vision." From the outset, Stevens' humor, irony, and imagery undercut the traditional romantic seriousness of the quest and the search for correspondence and meaning. Stevens plays with and undermines the genre, just as he "undermines" Crispin himself: "Crispin is 'unnamed.' There is no longer any clear 'word' to define him. Not only has he been poetically reduced to 'nothing himself' but the fictions which surround him, those that would establish the nature of the Crispin-quester figure, have been de-created and their efficacy put in doubt" (Bové 201). Crispin's "reduction," however, leads not to comfort or finality but rather to further and further searchings through metaphoric distortion. Chance is all that finally "ends" Crispin's wanderings, settling him in domestic in-ertia. But even there he recognizes the enervating trap of stasis.

Crispin never learns that "all structures are fictions and man-made for the relief of tension and anxiety" (Bové 205). Stevens' ending itself is playfully ironic, sub-verting any sense of conclusion or closure. But Stevens (and Crispin) *have*, Bové thinks, been successful in their "failed quest": "Crispin proves himself to be nothing. He proves nothing to be at the center. Most importantly, as a poetic device, he proves nothing in two senses: he shows no finality in the working out of his story—as a poetic device he proves to be nothing of final value; yet, as a device, what he does positively prove or confirm 'Is nothing.' He demonstrates to the reader and poet the truth of 'The Snow Man.' All of what-is shares in nothingness" (Bové 206).

Despite attempts to refine and redefine their engage-ment with Stevens, the deconstructive critics fell under the censure of yet another critic attempting to define a new direction for critical study. Frank Lentricchia in *After the New Criticism* attempts to illuminate the prob-lems of a number of directions in modern criticism, many of which use versions of Stevens to ground their arguments. Among these, the techniques of poststruc-turalist American critics receive Lentricchia's saltiest indictments for their reprivileging of literary discourse, their devices of "new formalism" and "hedonist" aesthetics, their various uses of the concept of "abyss" (or "nothingness") as an inverse ontological ground and as a new totalizing "center" for critical discourse, and finally, their ahistoricization of literature and language.

Early in his own career, Lentricchia had engaged the poetry and poetics of Wallace Stevens to new ends in *The Gaiety of Language: An Essay on the Radical Poetics of W. B. Yeats and Wallace Stevens.* His use of Stevens here, the stance of his early polemics, and the subsequent changes in his treatment of the poet reveal much about the growth of a historicist theory which raises its voice against the major contemporary directions in criticism. Lentricchia in the midsixties found himself facing conflicting contexts in criticism—specifically, conflicting views of Wallace Stevens. On the one hand, the New Critics' "contextual" theory of the autonomy of the artwork saw modern poetry as effecting a radical break with its romantic heritage; on the other, a critical suspicion of "self-sufficiency theories" revealed New Critical tendencies to be simply "restatements of Coleridgean poetic" and viewed modern poetry as an ongoing illustration of the romantic legacy. But given a choice between "antiromantic" formalism and the "romanticist" views of visionary poetics (including those of Harold Bloom), Lentricchia asserts that "neither alternative is adequate" to account for the "radical poetics" of Wallace Stevens (Lentricchia, *Gaiety* 1).

In *The Gaiety of Language,* Lentricchia cites his opponents by name—J. Hillis Miller, Roy Harvey Pearce,

Harold Bloom, and Joseph Riddel—and as an alternative to their then-current theories of Stevens as "philosophical poet," modern humanist, or visionary romantic, Lentricchia posits Stevens the "fictionalist," the "impure" Burkean ironist who wavers in an "unresolved dialectic" between the yes of transcendent desire and the no of his factive naturalism. Throughout much of the study, Lentricchia carefully severs the presumed ties between the romantic aesthetic and the poetics of Stevens, declaring him to be a poet who precludes nineteenth-century idealism through his awareness of the finite imagination, an awareness which allows his "escapism" through deliberate fictions to remain nonetheless rooted in the strictures of the "real." In the end, moreover, Lentricchia's theory of the "poetics of will" points in an important historical direction which might wrest Stevens from both contextualism and romanticism and which informs the bulk of Lentricchia's future criticism. Here an excerpt from the concluding pages illustrates the already-present emphasis on historicism:

> The poetics of will defines the imagination as a finite energy that seeks to ground itself in the linguistic medium, and isolates poems as the artifacts of the private self operating in a particular place at a particular time. The role of the poet is that of shaper or maker: the poet is not a seer or a "representative," symbolic figure; the poem is not a symbol for another reality. The continuum of nature has been fragmented. Consequently, Yeats and Stevens invite rather than discourage historical probing as they place themselves in Camus's world of "irrational bitterness," a "semi-world" with no transcendental com-

pletion. Their acceptance of the naturalistic and even existential schemes of the world of experience puts poetry irrevocably back into time. (Lentricchia, *Gaiety* 189)

This existential, self-consciously fictional Stevens re-emerges in *After the New Criticism* as the central man of "post-Kantian" aesthetic theory grounded on a radical self-consciousness of the poetic act. Stevens' irony appears to point the way toward a strategic break from theoretical modes dominating the critical scene, just as in *The Gaiety of Language,* the "poetics of will" allowed Lentricchia an avenue by which to circumvent New Criticism and "visionary" romanticism. In *After the New Criticism,* however, the "radical poetics" of the prior Stevens have become a "conservative" fictionalism, an avenue which is here shown to lead, not to a break with the prevailing formalist aestheticism or with myth-criticism's "grander aestheticism" but to a cul-de-sac harboring its own "guilty aestheticism," incorporating the most insidious elements of isolationism, hedonism, and moral relativism.

Lentricchia summarizes the currency of the "fictionalist" tendency in modern criticism and Stevens' immense impact on the course of modern theory. During the 1960s, the American theoretical avant-garde

was beginning to become fascinated with Wallace Stevens, and soon the language of fictionalism was to displace the language of myth criticism. . . .

It is . . . difficult to overestimate the vogue of Wallace Stevens in the 1960s. No young academic coming out of graduate school in the middle of the decade with an ad-

vanced degree in literature could claim critical sophistication unless he could discourse knowingly, off the
cuff, on "supreme fictions," the "gaiety of language,"
and the "dialectic of imagination and reality." No mature
intellectual could be comfortable unless he could move
smoothly into such ponderous conversation. Not long
after the poet's death in 1955 the Stevens industry began
to prosper such that it eventually swallowed whole all
competition in the criticism of modern poetry. (Lentricchia, *ANC* 30)

Lentricchia, self-parodically astute, once just such a
"young academic" (with his revised Duke University dissertation, *The Gaiety of Language,* as membership card in
the Stevens vogue), now extracts himself firmly from
both the nominal source and the eventual course of such
criticism.

Stevens' "fictionalism"—earlier a token of authenticity, a type of good faith, a "gaiety" in spite of (or because of) the provisional freedoms of language and the
poet's own scrupulous self-awareness—now becomes
"paranoid," a "perilous" and "schizoid" tendency, an agonized "last-ditch humanism" (Lentricchia, *ANC* 33,
241, 33) in the terrible face of modern nihilism. The
concept of reality as "other," once the vehicle for Stevens' rupture with romantic idealism and the hitching
post to which he tied the imagination, now bears the epithet of "inhuman chaos," the "sure engulfment, madness, and death," the existential horror which, when
"privileged," can (and does) reveal our creations to be
"pitifully unheroic lies" (Lentricchia, *ANC* 33). In all,
"Stevens's dominant tendency to align truth and reality

155

with an inhuman chaos 'outside' human consciousness and human discourse produces an antipoetics whose constant lament and wearisome message is the futility of all human effort" (Lentricchia, *ANC* 33).

Beginning from this "mortal no," Lentricchia traces the dilemma of the fictionalist aesthetic in the works of Frank Kermode, who, with Murray Krieger, he considers to be in a theoretically filial relationship to Stevens, ranked among the members of "a post-Kantian line which, in its ultimate extension in Sartre, concludes in an odd mixture of Kantian and anti-Kantian themes" (Lentricchia, *ANC* 31). Lentricchia takes issue with the "obsessive" dualism established in post-Kantian theory and traces the ramifications of the antitheses of fiction and reality as they have evolved from Kant and Nietzsche through Sartre, Vaihinger, and Kermode. One aspect of that dualism is the implicit trivialization of fiction: Kant, in separating fiction from any cognitive function or ontological status, in Lentricchia's assessment, "became the philosophical father of an enervating aestheticism which ultimately subverts what it would celebrate" (Lentricchia, *ANC* 41). The self-consciousness of fictionality here becomes that capacity for reminding ourselves of the impotence of our own imagination, its arbitrariness and severance from the "real" world. What results from this recognition, Lentricchia asserts, is a "dialectic of guilt and desire"—an oscillating movement toward the trivial but necessary comforts of fiction (which we desire), balanced by a guilty return to the real world (in which we cannot abide)—the agonized movement of which pervades the poetics of conservative fictionalism.

156

Permeating this dualism Lentricchia perceives is an inveterate privileging of "the real," involving a turn toward ontology which both compounds the trivialization of fiction and leads to an ultimate dilemma in the fictionalist tradition. In the early works of Nietzsche, this turn takes the form of the Dionysian judgment accorded privilege over the Apollonian "veils" of fiction, since the former "comes from being" and is rooted in "the core of things." Sartre, too, in Lentricchia's detailed analysis, reveals himself to be a "secret ontologist" who rhetorically gives prominence to nonhuman being over the human consciousness (the *en-soi* over the *pour-soi*), and so "appears to reprivilege that world behind the scene which with Nietzsche he had thought to have forever banished" (Lentricchia, *ANC* 45).

Nonetheless, Sartre sees the imagination as a temporary freedom from life, and it is this further aspect of the fiction/reality dualism which Lentricchia pinpoints as a thinly veiled *contemptus mundi* aestheticism. Despite the preeminence of "being" for these theorists, the world is consistently seen as horrible, and this attitude Lentricchia repeatedly diagnoses as paranoia. For Stevens the world is "a 'violence' which presses in upon us; a 'preposterous pig' which must be remade, 'lock, stock, and barrel,' according to W. B. Yeats; a 'black and utter chaos,' in the words of Robert Frost" (Lentricchia, *ANC* 53). For Hans Vaihinger, the real consists of a "hostile external world" which "assaults" the human consciousness (Lentricchia, *ANC* 53). And even in Sartre, for whom consciousness of the real brings on nausea, Lentricchia perceives, in the end "the existential-phenomenological rhetoric of this Continental philosopher cannot mask the constant theme of the conservative fictionalist who would like to leave the living to the servants, but who couldn't respect himself if he did" (Lentricchia, *ANC* 53). Not only does this attitude suggest guilt and paranoia to Lentricchia, but true to the delusions about the grandiose self which are characteristic of that pathology, it suggests a perverse elitism, an "arrogance," and the self-congratulatory, self-pitying cultivation of a "myth of chaos" which then bestows on the act of "form-making" an "ultimate value" and on the modern artist the limelight of agonized triumph (Lentricchia, *ANC* 55).

All in all, Lentricchia indicts Stevens' legacy of "conservative fictionalism" as perpetrating a duality leading to elitism, isolationism, and inactivity—an inactivity which bears with it the effect of a laconic evasion of moral responsibility in the real world. Fictionalism's "guilty aestheticism," moreover, violates its own theoretical integrity by attempting the "magical" sleight-of-hand mediating between fiction and reality, forgetting in its inadvertent slip into ontology the violation of its own premises by trying to transcend its own dualism. This attempt demonstrates, for Lentricchia, an uncritically presence-oriented, implicitly metaphysical stance, one unaware, finally, that its own foundation of antithesis "is itself a construction" (Lentricchia, *ANC* 60).

Lentricchia's crusade against aestheticism runs deep; he decries it as a stance at once theoretically infirm, morally relativistic and nihilistic, and most important, as an obstacle to understanding literature in its fully temporal, fully historical light. Stevens himself, once seen as

158

returning the poetic act to time, has now become co-conspirator in an atemporalizing aestheticism pervasive throughout modern criticism. Moreover, Stevens plays a role in Lentricchia's critique of poststructuralism in a chapter offering two bold alternatives to contemporary criticism: "History or the Abyss."

That essay begins by reiterating Stevens' impact on the modern critical tendency toward (or inability to evade) privileging the literary realm (Lentricchia, *ANC* 158) and later places Stevens centrally in the advent of deconstructive criticism in America. It was, Lentricchia argues, to a large extent J. Hillis Miller who ushered the theories of Derrida into the American intellectual scene of the early seventies, by way of critical reviews and attacks and a major two-part essay on Wallace Stevens ("Stevens' Rock and Criticism as Cure," *Georgia Review* 30, 1 & 2 [1976]). It was a time when Miller "assumed the burden of chief spokesman and polemicist" for deconstruction in America and "carried Stevens into the poststructuralist camp" (Lentricchia, *ANC* 162). But Lentricchia's unspoken assumption seems to be that Stevens' abduction (notably from the New Critical camp) was not at all difficult, given the odd similarities Lentricchia seeks to demonstrate between modernist formalism and postmodernism's segue into the "ultimate formalism." Implicitly, through Stevens, the connection is already suggested, much being revealed about links among critical schools by the poetic company they keep, and Lentricchia isolates Stevens as an alluring model for and invitation to critical aestheticism.

Lentricchia goes on to analyze systematically the prob-

lems inherent in the "Yale school" of Derridean critics
(Lentricchia names J. Hillis Miller, Paul de Man, and
Geoffrey Hartman as practitioners) and their falling-off
from a trend toward historicism in Derrida's writing
which Lentricchia would resurrect. He begins by identifying an implicit and pervasive "new hedonism" in the
writings of the Yale Derrideans, brought about by the
misuse of the concepts of freedom and play suggested
by the deconstructive principle of decentering. "Terms
like 'joy' and 'activity,' and their variants, are fundamental" in the work of the Yale critics. "They recall the overt
preoccupations of the nineteenth-century aesthetes with
a *telos* of 'pleasure' and a quest for 'freedom' that have
typified an astonishing variety of modern critical theories whose presuppositions are idealistic (in the Kantian
sense) and whose critical practices are disposed toward
one sort of formalism or another" (Lentricchia, *ANC*
169). Yet in actuality, Lentricchia claims: "The fundamental aspects of Derrida's writing plainly do not sanc-
tion a new formalism or a new hedonism, but the Yale
appropriation of him . . . is just as plainly an ultimate
formalism, a New Criticism denied its ontological supports and cultural goals. . . . The Yale Derrideans will
not in the long run threaten every partisan of tradi-
tionalism, because they will turn out to be tradi-
tionalism's last formalist buttress" (Lentricchia, *ANC*
169).

Not only does Lentricchia indict these critics on the
grounds of pervasive formalism, he also detects an underlying ontology in their use of Derrida's second central
concept, "differance." Whereas "Derrida is no ontologist

of *le néant* because he is no ontologist," and the concept of differance stands as "the subversion of all ontological versions of the center" (Lentricchia, *ANC* 171), Lentricchia claims that the figure employed throughout the writing of the Yale Derrideans, that of *mise en abyme*, becomes itself a "new center" and a new ontological grounding: "Though Derrida warned that differance, as the subversion of all ontological realms, could authoritatively command nothing, the Yale critics have taken differance as a radically subversive authority which autocratically commands, as *abyme*, the whole field of writing, and while doing so establishes writing as a monolith itself that forever escapes determination" (Lentricchia, *ANC* 173).

In opposition to the Yale appropriation of Derrida into a new formalism and a new authority which privileges the literary text, Lentricchia employs Derrida in a new direction, positing a Derridean theory of historicity which sharply contrasts with the Yale formalism:

> Put as baldly as possible, Derrida's point [in his proposal to shift the philosophical focus from self-present speech to writing] is that once we have turned away from various ontological centerings of writing, we do not turn to free-play in the blue, as the Yale formalists have done. Rather, it would appear that our historical labors have just begun. . . .
>
> Consciousness, the subject, the presence or absence of being, apparently forever dissolved as versions of the untouchable transcendental signified, now suddenly return as they all become situated as intertextual functions of semiological systems which do recognize the "rights of

history, production, institutions" to coerce and constrain the shapes of free-playing discourse. Semiological systems based on the principle of difference "have been produced," and the key questions become what and by whom. . . . If Derrida concludes the project of Nietzsche . . . then he also suggests the initiation of a new project (in this sense he has surely known exactly where he is going), a project already handsomely underway in the poststructuralist writings of Michel Foucault: to uncover the nonontological reincarceration of the signifier within cultural matrices which, though themselves subject to difference and change, nevertheless in their moment of power, use the signifier, take hold of it, establish dominance over it. (Lentricchia, *ANC* 175–76)

Lentricchia's attempt to rescue Derrida from the Derrideans (just as in Part II of *After the New Criticism* he attempts to rescue Harold Bloom from Harold Bloom) is a powerful effort in the interests of historical consciousness to claim the field from the deconstructive critics. Joseph Riddel, however, was one who rallied to a rebuttal, in which he sought not only to demonstrate the continuing stronghold of deconstruction but its reach and scope as well. And as so often before, the subject for study was Wallace Stevens—a casualty in Lentricchia's battle for historicity now enthusiastically reenlisted in the continuing war of critical appropriation.

Riddel's polemic, spearheading a 1983 special issue of *The Wallace Stevens Journal*, "Stevens and Postmodern Criticism," discusses the general clamor over and mistrust of deconstructive criticism and in particular its appropriation of Wallace Stevens. He cites the attempts by such critics as Harold Bloom to make of Stevens a subversive weapon against that movement, using him as "the eternally American answer to European negative theology, and hence to 'deconstruction'" (Riddel, "Climate" 60). Nonetheless, "it was not until Frank Lentricchia's *After the New Criticism* that there has been any serious attempt to dislodge Stevens from the eccentric center of what some call post-modernism" (Riddel, "Climate" 60). Riddel's project in this essay elects to be a neutral one, "to trace out the variety of climatic vortices into which Stevens' poetry had been swept, and to suggest why, more than any other modernist poet, he has been made to stand at the crossroads of contemporary criticism" (Riddel, "Climate" 60). But the essay quickly abandons neutrality in favor of a strong critique of Lentricchia and an equally aggressive reemphasis of deconstruction's all-encompassing tenets.

Riddel's dismissal of Lentricchia's position centers on a number of points, some more credibly argued than others. In general, Riddel indicts Lentricchia for succumbing to a kind of Winturgian moralism and dogmatism, for implicitly validating a literary history that privileges the literary imagination over "the world," even for being a surrogate romantic himself in his definitions of a "responsible poetic language." Riddel attempts to show the reductiveness of Lentricchia's discussion of the "Yale formalists," first by broadening the clientele of that group to demonstrate that Stevens is by no means "central" to that (itself quite fluid) "school," then by illustrating the variety of "Stevenses" that the Yale critics Bloom, Hartman, and Miller in fact employ.

For Riddel, Lentricchia's depiction of "the so-called new-est 'Yale School'"

> necessarily discounts Paul de Man, whose literary mod-els remain largely European . . . and Jacques Derrida, who if he has heard of Stevens at all may think of him only as an American Mallarmé. And since Derrida and de Man are the theoretical core of the school, and only Miller among the doctrinaire "deconstructionists" em-ploys Stevens as a central metaphorician, as it were, such histories [as Lentricchia's] of "schools" not yet accredited are at best useful for polemics.
>
> In other words, the Stevens on whom Lentricchia cen-ters the entire modern history of an abysmal nihilism, Stevens the aesthete, is hardly the one who turns up as a paradigm for the two major proponents of deconstruc-tive criticism, and as for the other three, Stevens would seem to be at least four different poets: 1. the Gnostic poet of Bloom, who passes through the negative or skep-tical abyss—which Bloom misconstrues as the decon-structive moment—in order to signify the "transumption" or overcoming that is America's and Emerson's answer to Europe and Nietzsche; 2. Hartman's provider of meta-phors for the ultimate privilege of poetic warmth over philosophical coldness; 3. Miller's "sure questioner" sus-pended over the abyss of language who nevertheless of-fers us a "cure" for criticism's appetite to retrieve truth or knowledge from poetry, thereby making poetry a certain kind of undeceived discourse; 4. that Stevens who for all three signifies the privilege of poetry to philosophy and who can thus provide the critique for all extant literary theories while offering a medium out of which to fash-ion a new one. (Riddel, "Climate" 62–63)

This "new theory" for Riddel is one which must paradoxically undermine itself, must be "at once a methodical strategy for opening a reading and an interference with or disruption of method . . . the disturbance in every reading which begins to attend to the way language breaks its own laws" (Riddel, "Climate" 66). Moreover, Riddel sees the project of deconstruction as not so much to reread the poet "correctly" but in fact to contest the authoritative "correctness" of any critical reading, to "challenge the claims of other methods to read him properly" (Riddel, "Climate" 66). Riddel's claim is that by virtue of the nature of language, both literary and critical, all texts are "already self-deconstructions" which undo and create, disrupting closure in themselves as well as engaging in the "dis-semic" play of meaning occasioned by that rupture. And deconstruction as a critical act "keeps pointing up those moments when the illusion of self-reflexivity in a text breaks down, whether upon an undecidable sign or a rhetorical crux, and where in this catachresis a play takes over" (Riddel, "Climate" 67). Finally, regarding the conventional desire for explicative meaning and truth in Stevens criticism, deconstruction "can only remind us that such closures belong not to the poems, which are readings themselves, but to the readings of the poems which have grown tired of Stevens' challenge to, if not lack of, seriousness" (Riddel, "Climate" 68).

As a program for redefining and broadening the deconstructive enterprise to disclaim its accruing notoriety as "a purely textual practice which repeatedly arrives at the same conclusion" or as "just another version of the old [aesthetic, formalist] structure" or even as "a reading program or strategy adapted to certain kinds of texts" (Riddel, "Climate" 63, 65), Riddel's polemic is not altogether successful, especially inasmuch as he concludes his essay with an explication of Stevens' "Credences of Summer" which, though an excellently wrought exercise in figural analysis, does not altogether escape Lentricchia's earlier charges of formalist tendencies in deconstruction. Moreover, as a critique of Lentricchia's historicist position, Riddel's essay merely dismisses the very crux and motive of Lentricchia's argument as a "blindness" and "frosty impasse," as yet another of many mystified critical searches for "an adequate external language . . . that opens up or frees the creative or internal language of the poem even as it effaces itself" (Riddel, "Climate" 64). Thus, Riddel appears to overlook Lentricchia's more complicated adherence to the theories of Michel Foucault, particularly his self-aware historicism, which posits the exploration of "cultural matrices" rather than any autotelic "internal language," and the attempt to situate the critic within the latter's own historical discourse, a discourse presumably not "self-effacing" at all but hermeneutically aware.

But if Riddel's essay might not itself undermine Lentricchia's call for a historically oriented criticism, the ongoing production of deconstructive versions of Wallace Stevens attests to the continuation of that method and its attraction to the "linguistic and textual tangle" of such a poet. Nor has the field of critical dissent been narrowed to the two combatants, "History or the Abyss."

Into the Eighties

A recent collection of essays edited by Albert Gelpi, *Wallace Stevens: The Poetics of Modernism* (1985), attests to a newly complicated faceting of this major modern poet, moving between and beyond the larger theoretical battles of strong reading, existential phenomenology, deconstruction, and historicism.

Gelpi's motives for compiling the collection, articulated in his preface, present an ambitious but somewhat misleading introduction to these essays. As part of his proposal he suggests that

> one of the purposes of this collection is to present in concert six critics of twentieth-century poetry who have not previously published much, if anything, about Stevens—critics who are not, in any case, members of the Stevens critical establishment. His work has rightly commanded the attention of some of our ablest critics, particularly since the fifties, and the results have been extremely illuminating. But in the process something of a consensus approach has emerged, concentrated on explicating the strategies for fictionalizing the interaction of the imagination and reality into poems. The essays in this volume hope to contribute to a new phase of Stevens criticism from a number of intersecting and overlapping perspectives. (Gelpi vii)

Despite the suggested disinterest of these critics, however, and their presumed antiestablishment "innocence," each moves well within the boundaries of "established" Stevens criticism—not because of any narrowness of approach but because of the reach of Stevens criticism and its incorporation of the major theoretical polemics of the day. It is a field which hardly evinces the "consensus

167

approach" Gelpi so easily suggests. In the end, the "new phase of Stevens criticism" to be inaugurated and illustrated through these essays, in all its eclecticism, still reflects in central (though undisputably innovative) ways advances and refinements of preexisting theoretical struggles which have dominated Stevens studies.

Michael Davidson's essay, "Notes Beyond the *Notes:* Wallace Stevens and Contemporary Poetics," is an excellent example of an analysis which acknowledges and incorporates, while it attempts to move beyond, such landmarks of Stevens criticism as Bloom's theories of influence and the romantic element in Stevens, Bové's hermeneutics, the insights of the Yale deconstructors, and the contemporary move toward historical criticism. Davidson opens by asserting the influence of Stevens on Charles Olson's central postmodern concept of "Projective Verse," by way of Robert Creeley's admiration and use of Stevens' poetics. Davidson sees Stevens as having provided for this group of postmodern poets a version of the romantic organicist theory which could circumvent the problems of "Kantian disinterestedness" and the New Critical preoccupation with "autotelic form." As an alternative, Stevens "reintroduced into theories of Romanticism what Coleridge elsewhere calls 'form as proceeding,' that might serve as a paradigm for more recent open-ended and processual modes" (Gelpi 142). In light of this thesis, Davidson's essay seeks to explore Stevens' three contributions to postmodern poetics: "the use of the long poem in producing a destructive or decreative poetics; the operational or performative use of language to create a philosophical poetry; and the transformation, by these means, of a poetry of 'place' into a poetry of 'occasions'" (Gelpi 144).

Davidson's application of Stevens to the postmodern poetic enterprise must address—and, as Davidson does, either appropriate or dismantle—previously monolithic figures in Stevens criticism. Justifying his own venture into an analysis of influence (here Stevens' "bounty" traced in the works of postmodern poets like Robert Creeley, John Ashbery, and Michael Palmer), Davidson takes issue with Harold Bloom's "psychopathological" mechanism of poetic heritage. Significantly, he invokes both Paul Bové and Frank Lentricchia as polemical supports for his criticism of Bloom's having "severely limited the contextual field in which we may read literary history" and his having created a theory which "limits the kind and scope of influence to those poets who most resemble [Stevens] at the level of rhetorical surface" (Gelpi 143–44). In clearing a wider field for his own investigations, however, Davidson offers no alternative "theory," but merely an "alternative reading"—simply "a study of elements in Stevens' poetics that have helped generate at least one tradition in postwar poetry" (Gelpi 144).

Addressing Stevens' contributions to the destructive nature of the contemporary long poem, Davidson employs the findings of such theorists as Bové and the insights of hermeneutic criticism in Stevens studies, appropriating their concepts of Stevens' revisions of the romantic crisis poem and their use of Heidegger to articulate the concept of language as "generative," as "existential disclosure" of the temporality of being, thus anticipating in Stevens the postmodern move into a poetics "destructive" of both literary and philosophical stabilities. Through the "open-ended, processual style" shown in Stevens' long poems, "the poet is thus able to step beyond the closed, spatial text of high Modernism into a more speculative, temporarily generative text whose end is not literary history but existential disclosure. As a philosophical project, the authentically Postmodern poem dis-covers *(aletheia)* or uncovers the temporal nature of Being" (Gelpi 146). Davidson, however, focuses the hermeneutical stance on the project of *reading* rather than on writing, expanding the ramifications of Stevens' "generative text" in new directions which are taken up elsewhere in this collection, in Charles Altieri's essay on Stevens and the nature of modernist abstraction.

Davidson also pursues the concept of Stevens' "performative" language, bringing J. L. Austin's concept under the service of rhetorical analysis and employing as an illustration a commentary on Stevens by Yale critic Geoffrey Hartman which, in its striking resemblance to formalist textual analysis, cannot help but evoke echoes of Lentricchia's earlier criticisms of that school. Here, however, both comment and concept are employed to new ends:

> What is more pertinent to our concern with the later poems is Stevens' treatment of language as a system—its acoustics, its syntax, its pragmatics—in dramatizing ideas. . . . When he titles a poem, "Le Monocle de Mon Oncle," as Geoffrey Hartman points out, he captures in the minute phonemic difference between two words

170

something of the larger semantic resonance of the poem—the ironic portrayal of the uncle, metonymically figured in his eyepiece. This kind of operative or performative use of language has had an increasingly important function for contemporary poets as a way of writing a poetry of ideas within the very terms that those ideas present. (Gelpi 149)

Analysis such as Hartman's, once easily employed in the formalist enterprise of illuminating the structural and rhetorical integrity of the poem, now illustrates a new view of the poet, one geared toward the use of active, "operative" language acts to dramatize a world of generative ideas, finding correlatives in a postmodern poetry which attempts to show "not the *results* of inquiry but the *processes*" (Gelpi 153).

With Davidson's third thesis, Stevens seems very nearly to return to a Bloomian paradigm of late romantic crisis and alienation, overcome through a new type of imaginative reintegration. Davidson speaks of Stevens' "central romantic theme of personal and spiritual alienation," aligned to his uses of poetic language: "The fall of man, so the familiar version goes, is a fall into a de-mythologized world, a world of neutral signs, in which an Adamic language of unmediated presence has been lost. . . . This alienation is both destructive and creative: In order to conceive of a place as 'ours,' we must destroy it as 'other' and naturalize it in our own terms. This act of transformation generates another kind of reality, 'the supreme fictions without which we are unable to conceive of [the world]'" (Gelpi 153–54). Davidson sees a parallel movement in the work of postmodern poets, whose similar sense of "not-at-homeness" and perception of a rift between language and meaning results in what appears to be poetry of place (the regionalism current among contemporary writers) but which subtly shares in Stevens' more "propositional landscapes" (Gelpi 154). Stevens' final contribution to postmodern poetics is here the integration of change and temporality which qualifies and reintegrates the local: "Place is the becoming conscious of more than place, transforming spatial reality into occasion" (Gelpi 156).

Davidson concludes his essay by situating Stevens "in the transition between Modernism and Postmodernism," pointing to his experimentation with language, his preoccupation with the poet's apprehension of the world, and his possession of something like postmodern self-awareness in a poetry "critical of its own ability to achieve a supreme fiction at the expense of the world, critical of language in service to a transcendental ideal" (Gelpi 157). On the other hand, Stevens is divorced from the "critical poetry" of later decades in being, Davidson believes, removed from social, political, and ideological conditions. Here the emphasis on historicizing the aesthetic act evokes striking parallels with Lentricchia's prior critique of the dangers of atemporal aestheticism. Davidson seems to agree that Stevens' "well-known difficulties in responding to the specific conditions of historical change reflect a willingness to uphold the barrier between aesthetic and material production" (Gelpi 157) and imply consequences similar to Lentricchia's views of moral relativism:

Into the Eighties

If "Life consists / Of propositions about life," as [Stevens] says in "Men Made Out of Words," there is the danger that all such propositions are equally valuable and that their origin is entirely monologic rather than part of human dialogue. It has been for later poets to take up the kind of propositional, philosophical poetry that Stevens began and direct it toward particular social and ideological forms.

. . . in undermining certain formalist models of high Modernism, [Postmodern poetry] has attempted to enlarge the dialogic and discursive possibilities of poetry. It has called into question the nature of the single, self-sufficient subject, while opening a dialogue with the reader as coproducer of the text. It has brought the material nature of its own creation into sharp focus, treating poetic language not as a separate, sacrosanct domain (the poetic function) but as a dimension of sign and thus a social product. (Gelpi 157–58)

Davidson's essay, as it moves in a pattern of disengagement from and engagement with such theorists as Bloom, Bové, Lentricchia and the perspectives they have presented in their arguments over Wallace Stevens, suggests that the "novelty" of this current criticism is qualified at best; more likely, it indicates the inevitable circulation of critical language within the boundaries of previous debate. This is not to imply that Davidson's insights prove illegitimate or unoriginal. The use of Stevens as a context through which to illuminate certain facets of contemporary poetry highlights interesting aspects of Stevens' own experiment with language, as it raises additional questions about the process of poetic inheritance. But editorial suggestions that these essays are not bound to "the Stevens critical establishment" reveal instead a continued competition with the palimpsest of previous critical rewritings. The polemics of "establishment" Stevens studies continue to inform and direct the resituating of this poet within the shifting context of modern poetics.

Two further essays in this volume illustrate the ongoing involvement with critical landmarks of the 1970s and 1980s. Davidson's suggestion of the ahistorical element in Stevens, echoing Lentricchia's critique of 1980, is more fully explored in Marjorie Perloff's essay "Revolving in Crystal: The Supreme Fiction and the Impasse of Modernist Lyric." Seemingly historically oriented, yet lacking conspicuous methodology, Perloff's analysis is a curious attempt to identify the "political and social context" of Stevens' "Notes toward a Supreme Fiction." Using a combination of correspondence, biography, publishing history, and an outline of wartime events occurring during the months when he was composing "Notes," Perloff indicts Stevens for his purported retreat from the monumental political events of his day, calling this major poem "a kind of antimeditation, fearful and evasive, whose elaborate and daunting rhetoric is designed to convince both poet and reader that, despite the daily headlines and radio bulletins, the real action takes place in the country of metaphor" (Gelpi 42). By choreographing the contrasts between "the dark summer of 1942, when the Germans were pressing against the eastern front and the fighting in the Pacific was heavy" (Gelpi 47) and Stevens' finicky design of the "perfect

174

geometric whole" of "Notes," Perloff moves to argue
Stevens' elitist aestheticism, his removal from "the pressure of reality" in favor of the rhetorical "purity" of poetry, and she broadens his dilemma to represent the
general "impasse of Modernist lyric."

Perloff invokes Mikhail Bakhtin's theory of the dialogic imagination to discriminate between the closed,
"monologic" lyric authority attributed to Stevens and
other High Modernist "aesthetes" and the "rupture in
the lyric paradigm" demonstrated by such collagelike
poetry as Ezra Pound's *Cantos*. In "Discourse in the
Novel," Bakhtin had employed his concept of the internal dialogization of discourse and its potential drama-
tization in literature to formulate a distinction between
the novel and the lyric—more specifically, to quote
Bakhtin, between "artistic prose" and those genres
which are "poetic in a narrow sense" (Bakhtin 284). The
former, in Bakhtin's paradigm, is identified by writing
which puts to use the "sense of the boundedness, the
historicity, the social determination and specificity" of
language through an interaction with "alien discourse,"
allowing the entry and play of multiple "languages"
within the work. The resultant effect of relativizing and
"de-privileging" any particular discourse sets such work
against more narrowly "poetic" writing which presumes
the direct, unmediated power of the artist's language to
assign meaning. In the latter stance, the artist assumes a
traditionally unified, monologic voice and views his language as authoritative, "a pure and direct expression of
his own intention" (Bakhtin 285).

Despite Bakhtin's discrimination among genres, Perloff's curiously swift critical segue asserts that "today we can apply this distinction to poetry itself" and appropriates the complex terms *monologic* and *heteroglossic* from Bakhtin's paradigm to separate what she terms the single-voiced "straight lyric" of such poets as Stevens from the multivocal "collage poetry of the Pound tradition." Pound and company, by inviting the entry of other, "impure" discourses into poetry, presumably achieve a type of self-historicization, an undermining of the polarity between "art" and "life."

Returning to Stevens, Perloff compares readings of "Notes" that span the careers of Harold Bloom and Joseph Riddel. Bloom, not surprisingly, is shown to emphasize the "heroic integration" of poetic humanism in an age of alienation (later in Bloom's career to become a dismissal of history and a more desperate turn to "the solitary self as mortal god" [Gelpi 56]). Riddel's early vision of Stevens' "humanistic myth" of the Major Man turns later to a deconstructive reading, which nonetheless still suggests to Perloff the desire to master repetition, to inaugurate the "man-hero" within the labyrinthine Theatre of Trope (Gelpi 58). Implying here an impasse not merely in the lyric but in its interpretations (even among critics as seemingly antithetical as Bloom and Riddel), Perloff offers a new direction for the analysis of "Notes," one "willing to ask not just *how* meanings are created in the poem but *why*" (Gelpi 58). In the figure of MacCullough, the Major Man, Perloff sees latent leanings toward racism, sexism, and fascism:

> Despite Stevens' disclaimer that "MacCullough is any name, any man," the name MacCullough obviously car-

ries particular overtones. . . . MacCullough is, of course, a good Wasp name; it is not, assuredly, Spitzer or Rahv or Borgese. Again, MacCullough connotes racial purity; unlike, say, MacSweeney, which is Scotch-Irish, it is not contaminated. Third, *the* MacCullough connotes masculinity, a strong "hard-headed clan," as Bloom puts it, with a tradition of prowess in combat—the very opposite, surely, of the feminine, the weaker vessel. Indeed, given the context of European fascism, the very naming of "the MacCullough" brings to mind the stereotype of Aryan purity, the master race. (Gelpi 59)

Moreover, Perloff claims that despite critical belief that "Notes" "works toward a dismantling of such terms as 'First Idea,' 'Major Man,' 'gold centre,' and 'amassing harmony' (Gelpi 60), Stevens is in fact "far from immersing himself in the flux" but is still nostalgically "reaching out for the First Idea, the Supreme Fiction" which he attempts to fix in the stasis of "crystal," so evading an engagement with the "normal" and the actual, with "impure" reality. The concept of the Supreme Fiction, finally, receives a censure similar to Lentricchia's indictment of fictionalist elitism and paranoia; poetry becomes a vehicle, however provisional, by which to evade history and elevate poetic language and the poetic self above the strictures and impurities of life.

A political critique of this nature, however, raises a number of questions about the integration of poetry into its nominally historical context. Does mere chronological simultaneity (June, 1942: the completion of the manuscript of "Notes" and the Battle of Midway) imply irresponsibility in art that does not explicitly acknowledge current events? Furthermore, if Perloff implies a connection between lyrical "purity" and the tendency to racial "purity"—seeing the monologic closedness of Stevens' verse as indicating a dangerous social and political solipsism as well—then how can this theory account for the poetry of Ezra Pound (whom Perloff champions), which, though demonstrating its supposed rhetorical commitment to "the world" of competing discourses and identities through its stylistic "heteroglossia," nonetheless can harbor even more explicit leanings toward anti-Semitism and fascism? Finally, a historicism which reduces history to political events and majority ideologies (themselves shaped by our situated reception of them) may easily evade the deeper considerations which theoretical historicism demands—concepts of temporality and situatedness, of interest and change, undeniably central concerns in Stevens' poetry.

Charles Altieri is another critic who questions the un-self-conscious application of historical ideology to literature, rebuking critics who demonstrate "too programmatic and generalized a commitment to these demystifying inquiries," who "perhaps suppress out of embarrassment any need to take responsibility for their own idealizations" (Gelpi 86). In his essay "Why Stevens Must Be Abstract; or, What a Poet Can Learn from Painting," Altieri suggests that as critics we "be more willing to listen to Stevens before we allow ourselves the pleasures of trying to be superior to him" (Gelpi 87). Although he claims his objections are directed toward the new historicist impulse in general, in a long footnote Altieri explains the dearth of current historicist studies of Stevens:

The criticism of Stevens has not yet taken up the arguments the new historicism poses. Nor can it, I suspect so long as it remains dominated by three attitudes, none of which is capable of describing the roles abstraction plays in his poetry or that his poetry might play in our lives. For example, Harold Bloom's Nietzschean Stevens in pursuit of an imperial self engages in dramas it is impossible to socialize at all. At the other extreme, the Stevens of Helen Vendler's *Part of Nature, Part of Us* (Cambridge, Mass.: Harvard Univ. Press, 1980) is all too typical of contemporary society's willingness to identify with the august imagination only when it is "checked, baffled, frustrated, and reproved." Finally, Joseph Riddel's Deconstructionist Stevens, who seeks "a writing that kills" by constantly disclosing the artifice in our fictions, never ceases from decreation long enough to adopt a stance one can demystify or, one must add, that society can care about as a fiction. (Gelpi 116)

Altieri's essay takes up the question of Stevens' poetic dictum "It must be abstract," analyzing the concept of modernist abstraction in painting and poetry as an "intensification" of the action both of viewing and of reading, an illustration of "our own powers" which emphasizes the temporal element in interpretation. Moving from an intricate and illuminating analysis of the process of abstraction, Altieri demonstrates the significance of the *as:* rhetorical producer of resemblances, which, among other effects, through the act of reading becomes a paradigm of human value-creation: "The *as* literally produces resemblances, affords shifts in the level of discourse, and allows us to entertain provisional sympathies with a variety of attitudes. We see our seeing of x as y. Within such self-consciousness, the abstract *as* refers directly to the way poetry crosses life, because it names the state of equivalence basic to all acts of valuing. Reading becomes a paradigmatic form for such valuing" (Gelpi 106). Altieri uses Wittgenstein as a context for Stevens, to further demonstrate the project and potential of modernist abstraction to mediate between poetry and life, between twentieth-century extremes of empiricism and idealism: "Wittgenstein and Stevens both elaborate a Modernist imperative whose quest for concreteness as a philosophical tool leads ultimately to locating an 'indefiniteness' at the core of human experience and then putting it 'correctly and unfalsified, into words.' . . . The theorizing of poetry becomes the theory of life by positing alternatives for both empiricist reductionism and Idealist ontologizing. The being of beings is simply a matter of how the I manipulates 'the intricate evasions of as'" (Gelpi 111).

Though Altieri seems to stage his argument in opposition to historicist critics "concerned with social analysis or the articulation of specific political interests," his theories of abstraction and reading move conceptually toward an engagement with time, the world, self, and society. At once personal and transpersonal, reading becomes "a form of attention to phenomena that so involves investments in both the text and the world that it also becomes a paradigm for certain attitudes toward the self" (Gelpi 113). Focusing on Stevens' "motif" of reading, Altieri overrides objections to solipsism, idealism, or escapism: "The emphasis is not on heroic creative acts that appropriate the world under some single synthetic compositional force. There are dreams of appropriation, but they project a greenest cone formed out of powers we all share, powers we can even imagine forming a community around. Reading has a teleology that runs counter to individualist self-assertions. More important, reading is not a monistic principle. It idealizes shared powers, which themselves depend on worlds at once as intractable as minerals and as fertile as the *as* can make them" (Gelpi 114). Concentrating on the nuance of modernist abstraction, Altieri affords a new perspective on the temporal and communal nature of Stevens' poetry.

With their variety of voices and concerns—in their very contradictions continuing the tradition of Stevens studies—the essays in this volume effectively complicate networks of influence and affiliation in the modernist enterprise, while extending and questioning existing theoretical debates in the realm of Stevens scholarship. As a project, the redefinition of modernism itself reflects the contemporary atmosphere of concern with principles of canon formation, a general critical climate which by its nature moves scholarship into a historically self-aware realm. And the illuminating of new resemblances in twentieth-century literature, in which Stevens plays so integral a part, may point to future rewritings of this poet: Stevens may well develop further in his figure as a theorist of reading, continuing the exploration of generative, performative models of literature and language for which Altieri demonstrates philosophical and humanistic outcomes, and with which Davidson illustrates the fluid, operative processes of language and thought continued in the postmodern poetic enterprise. Stevens may also occasion a fruitful reexamination by historicist critics and, by the very intractability and complexity of his poetics, necessitate a deeper scrutiny of the aims and methods of the historicist project, taking into account cultural and ideological matrices surrounding a poet's work, yet allowing for nuances of artistic involvement with temporality, change, and human situatedness in the twentieth century.

Wallace Stevens remains central in this century's ongoing critical dissent and exploration. His advocates and his opponents alike reveal the richness of his poetics, as they reveal ideological grounds of disagreement moving well beyond the boundaries of the poetic subject at hand. The complexity of Stevens' poetry, from the time of his emergence early in the century, has occasioned redefinition of modernism, of the poetic act, and of our own involvement in the project of interpretation and appropriation that continues to inform the scene of twentieth-century criticism.

Postscript

The history of controversy surrounding Wallace Stevens' placement in the American literary canon affords a remarkable diagram of the agonistic process of critical appropriation. Few authors' reputations have been so reflective both of the certified "new pluralism" in literary criticism today and of the less advertised but equally polemical "old" pluralism which has characterized American critical voices throughout the twentieth century. But more than illustrating a chronicle of twentieth-century critical perspectivism, Stevens' engagement by the critical schools and by major critics offers a glimpse into the issues and literary politics which motivate the critical act. Finding *the* Stevens is not the object of such examination. Rather, it is a question of revealing how the poet is used as a vehicle, as an agonistic tactic and prize in the sphere of much larger critical arguments.

Today more than ever the posture of self-evidence in criticism has been brought rigorously into question. The proliferation of theoretical viewpoints has made clear the interested nature of canon formation: by virtue of the nature of criticism itself, the processes of selection, interpretation, and evaluation of literary texts are exercises of appropriation and power. A new critical view may begin as a response to the pressure of a literature demanding interpretation—the demands of novelty or obscurity which resist the methods of prior critical institutions. Invariably, however, as this critical view becomes a revision of traditional perspective, it establishes new literary institutions and canons which in their turn govern our critical practice and become contexts to be revised by new approaches. Furthermore, texts and authors assume in time the position of prizes which must be "won" by newcomers to the critical scene. The "major" works and writers which a new criticism can successfully appropriate, recruit, or master serve to support its validity, and it becomes imperative for new theories to incorporate these texts, both as repositories of authority and as weapons for the displacement of previous theories.

Literary study today demands a reexamination of criticism as an enterprise implicated in its own historical, cultural, and institutional milieu, attended by its own desires and politics. Edward Said posed a series of questions in *The World, the Text, and the Critic* that may easily underwrite the project of self-reflective revisionism in contemporary critical analysis: "What is it that maintains texts inside reality? What keeps some of them current while others disappear? . . . What are the centers of diffusion by which texts circulate?" (Said 152–53). By focusing on the critical project itself, an overview of the appropriative process promises to redefine the very nature of the literary object as a historical and critical occasion, as "a monument, a cultural object sought after, fought over, possessed, rejected, achieved in time" (Said 153).

Beyond literary politics, moreover, a genealogy of Stevens' fluctuating reception among the critical schools illustrates the prevalence throughout the twentieth century of many theoretical issues active today, including questions of artistic accomplishment and humanistic involvement, questions of philosophical aridity and political complacency in Stevens' once-lush "country of metaphor," of nominalism and hedonism, of artifice and the search for reality, and the general questions of the poet's place in a kaleidoscopic American literary canon which appears to rearrange itself for each new critical view. Reexamining Stevens' critical heritage in this way not only affords a glimpse of the critical enterprise in action but brings to light a palimpsest of opinion on which our current versions of the poet may be merely the latest and by no means the last inscription.

Works Cited

Abrams, M. H., ed. *Literature and Belief: English Institute Essays—1957*. New York: Columbia University Press, 1958.

Aiken, Conrad. "The Ivory Tower I." *The New Republic* 19 (May 10, 1919), 58–60.

———. *Scepticisms: Notes on Contemporary Poetry*. New York: Alfred Knopf, 1919.

Alvarez, A. "Wallace Stevens: Platonic Poetry." In his *Stewards of Excellence: Studies in Modern English and American Poets*. New York: Scribner's, 1958, pp. 124–39.

Babbitt, Irving. *Literature and the American College*. New York: Houghton Mifflin, 1908.

Bakhtin, Mikhail M. *The Dialogic Imagination*. Edited by Michael Holquist. Austin: University of Texas Press, 1981.

Blackmur, R. P. "An Abstraction Blooded." *Partisan Review* 10 (May–June 1943), 297–301.

———. "The Composition in Nine Poets: 1937." In his *The Expense of Greatness*. Gloucester, Mass.: Peter Smith, 1958, pp. 199–223.

———. "Examples of Wallace Stevens." In his *The Double Agent*. New York: Arrow Press, 1935, pp. 68–102. First

186

Works Cited

printed in *The Hound and Horn* 5 (Jan.–March 1932), 223–55.

——. "Poetry and Sensibility: Some Rules of Thumb." *Poetry* 71, no. 5 (Feb. 1948), 271–76.

——. "The Substance That Prevails." *The Kenyon Review* 17, no. 1 (Winter 1955), 94–110.

Bloom, Harold. *Wallace Stevens: The Poems of Our Climate.* Ithaca: Cornell University Press, 1977.

Bodenheim, Maxwell. "Modern Poetry." *The Dial* 68 (Jan. 1920), 95–98.

Bookman 56 (Dec. 1923), 483.

Bové, Paul. *Destructive Poetics: Heidegger and Modern American Poetry.* New York: Columbia University Press, 1980.

Buttel, Robert. *The Making of "Harmonium."* Princeton: Princeton University Press, 1967.

Carruth, Hayden. "Without the Inventions of Sorrow." *Poetry* 85, no. 5 (Feb. 1955), 288–93.

"Chicago Poets and Poetry." *Minaret* 1 (Feb. 1916), 24–25.

Deutsch, Babette. *Poetry in Our Time.* New York: Henry Holt, 1952.

Doggett, Frank. "Wallace Stevens and the World We Know." *English Journal* 48, no. 7 (Oct. 1959), 365–73.

——. "Wallace Stevens' Later Poetry." *ELH* 25, no. 2 (June 1958), 137–54.

Donoghue, Denis. Review in *The New York Review of Books* 24 (Sept. 15, 1977), 39.

Duncan, Joseph E. *The Revival of Metaphysical Poetry: The History of a Style, 1800 to the Present.* Minneapolis: University of Minnesota Press, 1959.

Ehrenpreis, Irvin. *Wallace Stevens: A Critical Anthology.* Middlesex: Penguin, 1972.

Empson, William. "An American Poet." *The Listener* 49 (March 26, 1953), 521.

Works Cited

Fletcher, John Gould. Review in *The Chapbook* 2 (May 1920), 28–30.

———. "The Revival of Aestheticism." *Freeman* 8, no. 197 (Dec. 19, 1923), 355–56.

Frankenberg, Lloyd. *Pleasure Dome: On Reading Modern Poetry.* Boston: Houghton Mifflin, 1949.

Fraser, G. S. "The Aesthete and the Sensationalist." *Partisan Review* 12, no. 2 (Spring 1955), 265–71.

Gelpi, Albert, ed. *Wallace Stevens: The Poetics of Modernism.* Cambridge: Cambridge University Press, 1985.

Grattan, C. Hartley, ed. *The Critique of Humanism: A Symposium.* New York: Brewer & Warren, 1930.

Handy, William J. *Kant and the Southern New Critics.* Austin: University of Texas Press, 1963.

Heringman, Bernard. "The Critical Angel." *The Kenyon Review* 14, no. 3 (Summer 1952), 520–23.

Hoeveler, J. David, Jr. *The New Humanism: A Critique of Modern America, 1900–1940.* Charlottesville: University Press of Virginia, 1977.

Hoffman, Frederick J., Charles Allen, and Carolyn F. Ulrich. *The Little Magazine: A History and a Bibliography.* Princeton: Princeton University Press, 1947.

Holden, Raymond. "The World of Music." *The Measure* 4, no. 37 (March 1924), 17–18.

Holmes, John. "Five Modern Poets." *Virginia Quarterly Review* 12 (April 1936), 288–95.

Humphrey, Robert E. *Children of Fantasy: The First Rebels of Greenwich Village.* New York: John Wiley & Sons, 1978.

Jarrell, Randall. "The Collected Poems of Wallace Stevens." *Yale Review* 64, no. 3 (March 1955), 340–53.

Kermode, Frank. "Notes toward a Supreme Poetry." *The New York Times Book Review* (June 12, 1977), 9, 44.

Kreymborg, Alfred. *Our Singing Strength.* New York: Coward-McCann, 1929.

Works Cited

———. *Troubadour—an Autobiography.* New York: Boni & Liveright, 1925.

Lafferty, Michael. "Wallace Stevens, a Man of Two Worlds." *Historical Review of Berks County* 24, no. 4 (Fall 1959), 109–13, 130–32.

Lentricchia, Frank. *After the New Criticism.* Chicago: University of Chicago Press, 1980.

———. *The Gaiety of Language: An Essay on the Radical Poetics of W. B. Yeats and Wallace Stevens.* Berkeley: University of California Press, 1968.

Lowell, Robert. "Imagination and Reality." *The Nation* 164, no. 14 (April 5, 1947), 400–402.

Martz, Louis L. "The World of Wallace Stevens." In *Modern American Poetry: Focus Five.* Edited by B. Rajan. New York: Roy, 1950, 94–108.

Matthiessen, F. O. *The Responsibilities of the Critic.* New York: Oxford University Press, 1952.

Miller, J. Hillis. "Dismembering and Disremembering in Nietzsche's 'On Truth and Lies in a Nonmoral Sense.'" *boundary 2,* 9, no. 3 (Spring 1981), 41–54.

———. "Theoretical and Atheoretical in Stevens." In *Wallace Stevens: A Celebration.* Edited by Frank Doggett and Robert Buttel. Princeton: Princeton University Press, 1980, 274–85.

———. "Wallace Stevens' 'Poetry of Being.'" In *The Act of the Mind: Essays on the Poetry of Wallace Stevens.* Edited by J. Hillis Miller and Roy Harvey Pearce. Baltimore: Johns Hopkins University Press, 1965, 143–62.

Monroe, Harriet. "The Audience II." *Poetry* 5, no. 1 (Oct. 1914), 31–32.

———. "A Cavalier of Beauty." *Poetry* 23 (March 1924), 322–37.

———. "The Free Verse Movement in America." *English Journal* 13 (Dec. 1924), 691–705.

———. "Mr. Yeats and the Poetic Drama." *Poetry* 16 (1920), 32–38.

189

Moore, Marianne. *Predilections*. New York: Viking Press, 1955.

Munson, Gorham. "The Dandyism of Wallace Stevens." In his *Destinations: A Canvass of American Literature Since 1900*. New York: J. H. Sears, 1928, 75–89.

Norris, Christopher. *Deconstruction: Theory and Practice*. New York: Methuen, 1982.

O'Connor, William Van. "Tension and Structure of Poetry." *Sewanee Review* 51, no. 4 (Autumn 1943), 555–73.

Pearce, Roy Harvey. "The Poet as Person." *Yale Review* 41, no. 3 (March 1952), 421–40.

———. "Stevens Posthumous." *International Literary Annual* 2 (1959), 65–89.

———. "Toward Decreation: Stevens and the 'Theory of Poetry.'" In *Wallace Stevens: A Celebration*. Edited by Frank Doggett and Robert Buttel. Princeton: Princeton University Press, 1980, 286–307.

———. "Wallace Stevens: The Life of the Imagination." *PMLA* 66, no. 5 (Sept. 1951), 561–82.

Pearce, Roy Harvey, and Sigurd Burckhardt. "Poetry, Language, and the Condition of Modern Man." *Centennial Review of Arts and Sciences* 4 (1960), 1–31.

Perloff, Marjorie. "Pound/Stevens: Whose Era?" *New Literary History* 13, no. 3 (1982), 485–514.

Poggioli, Renato. *The Theory of the Avant-Garde*. Translated by Gerald Fitzgerald. Cambridge: Harvard University Press, 1968.

Pound, Ezra. "The Audience I." *Poetry* 5, no. 1 (Oct. 1914), 29–30.

———. *The Letters of Ezra Pound*. Edited by D. D. Paige. New York: Harcourt, Brace, 1950.

Powys, Llewelyn. "The Thirteenth Way." *The Dial* 77 (July 1924), 45–50.

Ransom, John Crowe. "The Concrete Universal: Observations on the Understanding of Poetry II." *The Kenyon Review* 17, no. 3 (Summer 1955), 383–407.

Works Cited

————. *The World's Body.* New York: Scribner's, 1938.

Riddel, Joseph. "The Authorship of Wallace Stevens' 'Of Poetic Truth.'" *Modern Language Notes* 76, no. 2 (Feb. 1961), 126–29.

————. "Bloom—a Commentary—Stevens." *The Wallace Stevens Journal* 1, no. 3/4 (Fall/Winter 1977), 111–19.

————. "The Climate of Our Poems." *The Wallace Stevens Journal* 7, no. 3/4 (Fall 1983), 59–75.

————. "The Contours of Stevens Criticism." *ELH* 31, no. 1 (March 1964), 106–38.

————. "Interpreting Stevens: An Essay on Poetry and Thinking." *boundary 2*, 1, no. 1 (1972), 79–97.

————. "Metaphoric Staging: Stevens' Beginning Again of the 'End of the Book.'" In *Wallace Stevens: A Celebration.* Edited by Frank Doggett and Robert Buttel. Princeton: Princeton University Press, 1980, 308–38.

————. "The Metaphysical Changes of Stevens' 'Esthetique du Mal.'" *Twentieth Century Literature* 7, no. 2 (July 1961), 64–80.

————. "'Poets' Politics': Wallace Stevens' 'Owl's Clover.'" *Modern Philology* 56, no. 1 (Nov. 1958), 118–32.

————. "Stevens' 'Peter Quince at the Clavier': Immortality as Form." *College English* 23, no. 4 (Jan. 1962), 307–9.

————. "Wallace Stevens' 'Notes toward a Supreme Fiction.'" *Wisconsin Studies in Contemporary Literature* 2 (Spring–Summer 1961), 20–42.

————. "Wallace Stevens' 'Visibility of Thought.'" *PMLA* 77 (Sept. 1962), 482–98.

Riding, Laura, and Robert Graves. *A Survey of Modernist Poetry.* London: William Heinemann, 1927.

Rooney, William Jay. "'Spelt from Sibyl's Leaves'—a Study in Contrasting Methods of Evaluation." *Journal of Aesthetics and Art Criticism* 13 (June 1955), 507–19.

Rosenfeld, Paul. *Men Seen: Twenty-four Modern Authors.* New York: Dial Press, 1925.

Works Cited

Said, Edward. *The World, the Text, and the Critic.* Cambridge: Harvard University Press, 1983.

Seiffert, Marjorie Allen. "The Intellectual Tropics." *Poetry* 23 (Dec. 1923), 154–60.

Smith, William. "Modern Poetry: Texture and Text." *Shenandoah* 6, no. 2 (Spring 1955), 6–16.

Smith, William Jay. *The Spectra Hoax.* Middletown, Conn.: Wesleyan University Press, 1961.

Stevens, Wallace. *The Collected Poems of Wallace Stevens.* New York: Alfred Knopf, 1982.

———. *Letters of Wallace Stevens.* Edited by Holly Stevens. New York: Alfred Knopf, 1966.

Sukenick, Ronald. "Misreading Bloom." *Partisan Review* 45, no. 4 (Fall 1978), 634–36.

Sypher, Wylie. "Connoisseur in Chaos: Wallace Stevens." *Partisan Review* 13, no. 1 (Winter 1946), 83–94.

Tashjian, Dickran. *William Carlos Williams and the American Scene, 1920–40.* New York: Whitney Museum of American Art, 1978.

Taupin, René. *The Influence of French Symbolism on Modern American Poetry.* Translated by William Pratt and Anne Rich Pratt. New York: AMS, 1985.

Untermeyer, Louis. "Five American Poets." *Yale Review* n.s. 14 (Oct. 1924), 156–61.

———. "The Ivory Tower II." *The New Republic* 19 (May 10 1919), 60–61.

Van Doren, Mark. "Poets and Wits." *The Nation* 117 (Oct. 10, 1923), 400–402.

Van Vechten, Carl. "Rogue Elephant in Porcelain." *Yale University Library Gazette* 38, no. 2 (Oct. 1962), 41–50.

Walton, Edna Lou. "Beyond the Wasteland." *The Nation* 133 (Sept. 9, 1931), 263–64.

Wilde, Alan. *Horizons of Assent: Modernism, Postmodernism, and the Ironic Imagination.* Baltimore: Johns Hopkins University Press, 1981.

Works Cited

Willard, Abbie F. *Wallace Stevens: The Poet and His Critics.* Chicago: American Library Association, 1978.

Williams, Ellen. *Harriet Monroe and the Poetry Renaissance.* Chicago: University of Illinois Press, 1977.

Williams, William Carlos. "Comment: Wallace Stevens." *Poetry* 87, no. 4 (Jan. 1956), 234–39.

Wilson, Edmund. "Wallace Stevens and E. E. Cummings." *The New Republic* 28 (March 19, 1924), 102–3.

Winters, Yvor. "Postscript to 'Wallace Stevens; or, The Hedonist's Progress.'" In his *On Modern Poets.* New York: Meridian Books, 1959, pp. 34–35.

———. "Wallace Stevens; or, The Hedonist's Progress." In his *The Anatomy of Nonsense.* Norfolk, Conn.: New Directions, 1943, 88–119.

Index

Index

Index

Graves, Alfred Percival, 21
Graves, Robert, 45, 48–50, 54

Hartman, Geoffrey, 160, 163, 164, 170–71. *See also* Yale Critics
Harvard Advocate, 4
Harvard University, 3, 4
Hecht, Ben, 26
Hegel, George Wilhelm Friedrich, 112
Heidegger, Martin, 122, 123, 143–44, 146, 169
Heringman, Bernard, 85–86
Herrick, Robert, 108
Historicism, 152, 153, 161, 162, 166, 167, 168, 172, 178, 179, 180, 182
Hoffman, Frederick J., 31
Holden, Raymond, 46
Holmes, John, 44
Hopkins, Gerard Manly, 78, 108

Imagism (Imagists), 9, 15, 28, 30, 32, 36, 38, 86
Irony: xiv, 40–56, 69, 71, 88, 94, 146, 150, 151, 154, 171; disjunctive irony, 66; metaphysical irony, 81; Romantic irony, 91; "ironic" criticism, 146; "mastered irony," 148; Burkean irony, 153

Jackson, Laura Riding. *See* Laura Riding
James, William, 58
Jarrell, Randall, xv, 89, 94–95, 99
Jepson, Edgar, 27
Johns, Orrick, 29
Johnson, Jack, 11
Josephson, Matthew, 11

Kant, Immanuel, 59, 65, 66, 83, 145, 154, 156, 160, 168

Keats, John, 4
Kenner, Hugh, 130, 132
Kennerly, Mitchell, 15
Kermode, Frank, xv, 131, 136–37, 156
Kierkegaard, Søren, 146, 148
Knopf, Alfred, 8, 29
Kreymborg, Alfred, 9, 13, 18, 26, 28–31, 33, 34, 35, 36, 38
Krieger, Murray, 156

Laforgue, Jules, 35, 52
Lear, Edward, 130
Ledoux, Louis Y., 21
Lentricchia, Frank, 151–62, 163–64, 166, 169, 170, 172, 173, 174, 177
Levinsky, "Battling," 11
Lewis, "Kid," 11
Lewis, Wyndham, 26
Lindsay, Vachel, 21, 25, 27
Little Review, The, 7, 16, 25, 32
Lowell, Amy, 16, 21, 26, 29
Lowell, Robert, xv, 77–78
Loy, Mina, 7, 28, 29

McAlmon, Robert, 12
MacKaye, Percy, 21
MacLeish, Archibald, 55, 60
Mallarmé, Stéphane, 164
Markham, Edwin, 21
Martz, Louis, 84–85, 97–99
Masters, Edgar Lee, 16
Mather, Frank Jewett, Jr., 10
Matthiessen, F. O., 94
Mayakovsky, Vladimir, 2
Meynell, Alice, 21
Miller, J. Hillis, xv, 103, 111–17, 118, 128, 129, 131, 152, 159, 160, 163, 164
Minaret, 27
Modern School, The, 32

Index

Index

Stevens, Wallace: "A Child Asleep in Its Own Life," 107; "A High-Toned Old Christian Woman," 91; "Anecdote of the Jar," 61, 91; "Arrival at the Waldorf," 79; *The Auroras of Autumn*, 92, 95, 106–07; "The Comedian as the Letter C," 87, 91, 150–51; "The Course of a Particular," 109; "Credences of Summer," 110, 166; "Cy Est Pourtraicte, Madame Ste Ursule, et Les Unze Mille Vierges," 12; "Domination of Black," 78–79; "The Emperor of Ice Cream," 69; "Esthétique du Mal," 78, 120, 126; "From a Junk," 8; *Harmonium*, 8, 32, 53, 68, 72, 87, 104; "Home Again," 8; *Ideas of Order*, 104; "June Book," 6; "Le Monocle de Mon Oncle," 170; "Little June Book," 6; *The Necessary Angel*, 85, 92; "Nomad Exquisite," 84; "Notes toward a Supreme Fiction," 72–73, 77, 104–05, 126, 174, 176–77; "The Man with the Blue Guitar," 87, 91; "Men Made Out of Words," 173; "The Motive for Metaphor," 83; "Of Modern Poetry," 120; "Owl's Clover," 119; *Owl's Clover*, 97; *Parts of a World*, 72, 88; "Peter Quince at the Clavier," 29, 89, 121; "Phases," 24, 27; "Primordia," 10; "The Red Fern," 84; "The Relations between Poetry and Painting," 103; "Sea Surface Full of Clouds," 82; "The Snow Man," 70, 127, 148–49, 151; "Sunday Morning," 24, 87, 90, 91; *Three Travelers Watch a Sunrise*, 24; "To an Old Philosopher in Rome," 95; *Transport to Summer*, 74, 88, 92; "The Well-Dressed Man with a Beard," 110

Structuralism, x, 78
Sukenick, Ronald, 136
Surrealism, 9
Symbolism, 9, 32, 34, 35, 132
Sypher, Wylie, 93–94

Tate, Allen, xv, 57, 59, 63, 65, 66, 82, 96
Taupin, René, 34
Tennyson, Alfred Lord, 4
Thackeray, William Makepeace, 5
Thayer, Scofield, 31, 32
Transition, 7
Trend, 6, 7, 8, 13, 14
Tzara, Tristan, 2

Ulrich, Carolyn F., 31
Untermeyer, Louis, x, 13–14, 18, 30, 35–41, 44, 45, 54

Vaihinger, Hans, 156, 157
Van Doren, Mark, 54
Van Gogh, Vincent, 10
Van Vechten, Carl, 7, 8, 12, 13
Vendler, Helen, 122, 124, 131, 146, 179
Vorticism, 2, 9, 15

Wallace Stevens Journal, The, 162
Walton, Edna Lou, 54–55
Wang An-Shih, 5
Warren, Robert Penn, 63
Watts, Harold H., 120
Weil, Simone, 103
Whack at Public Taste, A, 7
Wheelock, John Hall, 21
Whitman, Walt, 22, 23, 39, 41, 91, 133
Wilde, Alan, 66–67
Wilde, Oscar, 12
Wilkinson, Marguerite, 21

Index

About the Author

Melita Schaum is Assistant Professor of English, University of Michigan–Dearborn. She received her doctorate from the University of Notre Dame, her master's degree from Stanford University, and her bachelor's degree from the University of Notre Dame.